The Sailing Circle

19TH CENTURY SEAFARING WOMEN FROM NEW YORK

By
Joan Druett
and
Mary Anne Wallace

With an Introduction by
Lisa A. Norling

Three Village Historical Society & Cold Spring Harbor Whaling Museum
Long Island, New York

The Sailing Circle

19TH CENTURY SEAFARING WOMEN FROM NEW YORK

Copyright © 1995
Three Village Historical Society & Cold Spring Harbor Whaling Museum

Library of Congress Number 95-62369
ISBN O-9636361-1-1
Three Village Historian Volume XXXVI

The research, exhibition, publications, and public programs
associated with *The Sailing Circle* have been made possible
through generous public and private funding.

Public Funds

The National Endowment for the Humanities
The New York State Council on the Arts
The Suffolk County Office of Cultural Affairs

Corporate and Foundation Support

Patron Level:
Banbury Fund
Northrop Grumman

Supporter:
Cowles Charitable Trust

Contributors:
Atlantic Mutual Companies
Fleet Bank
Mobil Foundation
NYNEX

Front Cover: Mary Swift Jones c. 1850; the Rowland Children, Woodhull, Mary Emma and Henrietta; The *Atalanta* by William York
Back Cover: Illustration from *The Girl's Own Paper*, 1885.

A portrait of Mary Amelia Swift Jones inspired the research project that led up to the exhibition *The Sailing Circle: 19th Century Seafaring Women from New York*. The portrait and the first professional director of the Three Village Historical Society, Michele Morrisson, arrived on Long Island within two weeks of each other in the fall of 1991. The experiences of Mary Swift Jones, a twenty-four year old bride who went to sea with her husband in 1858 and her sister sailors raised many questions about these fascinating women.

In the meantime, Ann Gill, Director of the Cold Spring Harbor Whaling Museum since 1985, had collected materials on women who went to sea with their whaling captain husbands. A preliminary review of the topic revealed that limited research had been done to explore the lives of the Long Island whaling wives.

Foreword

Wishing to place Mary Swift Jones' portrait on exhibit to tell the story of this 19th century wife's experiences at sea, the Three Village Historical Society approached the Whaling Museum to see if the Museum would collaborate in comparing and contrasting the experience of Long Island women who accompanied their sea captain husbands on whaling ships with the experiences of women who went to sea on merchant vessels. So began a collaborative three year research project.

A $5,000 planning grant from the New York State Council on the Arts allowed the project to retain a Research Associate, Irene Meisel, to detail the social history perspective on women at sea and to place some of the Long Island women into that context. She did so with the help of two consulting historians, Dr. Lisa Norling, Assistant Professor of History at the University of Minnesota, and Dr. Margaret Creighton, Associate Pro-

fessor of History at Bates College. At the same time, volunteers from the Historical Society and Ina Katz, Curator of the Whaling Society Museum, communicated with historical organizations on Long Island and along Connecticut's shoreline requesting artifacts, documents, and materials relating to Long Island women at sea.

In the summer of 1993, Joan Druett, the authority on whaling wives, came to the United States from her New Zealand home on a lecture circuit, promoting her book *"She Was a Sister Sailor," Mary Brewster's Whaling Journals, 1845-1851*. Subsequently, the William Steeple Davis Trust in the village of Orient, Long Island awarded Ron Druett, Joan's husband, an "artist-in-residency" for the academic year 1994-1995, and so Druett joined the project team as a consultant and writer.

Major funding from the National Endowment for the Humanities in 1995 allowed for the implementation of research findings into a major exhibition with accompanying catalog and the inclusion of the Peter Klosky Design Group in the project team. Additional funding for the project was provided by the New York Council on the Arts, Suffolk County Office of Cultural Affairs with generous corporate and foundation sponsorship by Atlantic Mutual Companies, Banbury Fund, The Cowles Charitable Trust, Fleet Bank, Mobil Foundation, NYNEX, and Northrop Grumman Corporation.

Acknowledgments

Many people have contributed to the success of this project. The Society and the Museum would like to thank everyone involved for their time, knowledge, materials, or skills, all of which have been invaluable to the success of this project.

We thank the families of our seafaring women: Carol Collins; Betsy, George, and Peter Delforge; Mr. and Mrs. Henry Gardiner; Marion Hoffmire; Mr. & Mrs. Raymond Rowland Randall; Ruth Rowland Randall; Mrs. Bruce Southworth, Barbara and Beverly Tyler.

Contributing researchers include: Wesley Balla, Fred Bone, Alan Haeberle, Estelle Lockwood, Dr. Mary Malloy, Dr. Sherman Mills, Alice Ross, Barbara Russell, Betty Sanial, Beverly Tyler, and Mary Anne Wallace. Janette Faust and Barbara Tyler were indefatigable transcribers. Ron Druett has been kind enough to lend slides of his detailed paintings of 19th century seafaring life. The historian readers who gave focus to the research were Dr. Margaret Creighton, Susan Klaffky, Dr. Lisa Norling, Vivien Rose, Dr. Laurie Rush, and Dawn Rusho. The first presentation of our work was the March 1995 Symposium, *Sister Sailors*, which was made possible by the collaboration of the Long Island Studies Institute at Hofstra University, and we deeply appreciate the work of Dr. Natalie Naylor and her staff.

Installation of the exhibit was greatly eased with assistance from: Clayton Collier, Leighton Coleman III, Travis Eastman, Elizabeth Kaplan, Michael Leonardi, Daria Merwin, Franklin Neal, Carrie Neal, Margaret Olness, Dr. Larry Swanson, Beverly Tyler, Barbara Tyler, and Christine Wasko.

Many museums and historical societies were extremely helpful in answering research queries, and a number loaned objects for the exhibition. We would like to thank: Phyllis Dillon, Frederica Wachsberger, Diana Latham, Mickie McCormic, Eleanor Williams, and Charlotte Hanson of The Oysterponds Historical Society; Dr. Donald Boerum, Charles Leety, and Mina Van Cleef of The William Steeple Davis Trust; Wally Broege of the Suffolk County Historical Society; Lucy Butler and Will Phippen of the Peabody-Essex Museum; Laveta Emory and Ann Yonemura at the Smithsonian Institution's Arthur M. Sackler Gallery; and Andy German, Joe Gribbons, and Connie Stein of the Mystic Seaport Museum.

For curriculum writing and student involvement we thank the Three Village Central School District: Dr. Mary Barter, Dr. Joyce Flynn, Dr. Deborah Blair, Dan Comerford, Doug Elliot, Joe Flaherty and Joan Oshman. And finally, we thank our friends for their help and our families for their support: Belle and Arthur Barstow, David Bernstein, Anne Marie Daly, Tom Gill, Janette and Edmund Handley, Cassandra Neal, Jan and Gene Neiges, and John and Eileen Petsco.

Michele M. Morrisson
Director
Three Village Historical Society

Ann M. Gill
Executive Director
Cold Spring Harbor Whaling Museum

In 1872, the U.S. Census Office published the results of the ninth (1870) Federal population census, the first to provide a comprehensive listing of female as well as male occupations. Of the 56,663 sailors tabulated, not a single one was female. While this may reflect some editing on the part of the Census Office, the point was clear: only men, it was supposed, went to sea – indeed, only men were supposed to go to sea. Popular notion and statistical compendium alike did not acknowledge at the time the women who accompanied their husbands or fathers onboard sailing vessels. We don't know their exact numbers, but easily hundreds of such women set sail on coasting and deep-water commercial trips, fishing and whaling voyages throughout the nineteenth century and well into the twentieth. Yet, like the cen-

with contradiction that can tell us more generally about American women's lives and about maritime culture at important transitional moments.

The nineteenth-century "sister sailors" pose a paradox in part because they left home at the very time when "home" was becoming more female-identified and more idealized than ever before, and in part because they intruded into an all-male space at the very time American culture was divided along gender lines more sharply than ever before. By the mid-nineteenth century, popular slogans and song lyrics pronounced the charms of "Home Sweet Home," describing it as a "sanctuary" or an "oasis," claiming "Be it ever so humble, there's no place like home." Home was glorified and associated with refuge, married love, a nuclear

stable Home centered around a Wife and Mother was sharply at odds with the reality of most women's lives. For one thing, the insistent proclamations about "Home Sweet Home" and women's place within it increased in frequency and volume just at the time when women were actually leaving home in unprecedented numbers. Some traveled for their health or amusement, and others went for their education. Many left home to try to save the world, as missionaries, reformers, or educators; thousands more headed west with their families to start new lives in new territories; and perhaps the greatest number went out to find paying work in domestic service or in the new factories, shops, and offices of the rapidly expanding American economy.

THE SAILING CIRCLE
Introduction
by Lisa Norling

sus enumerators, both maritime historians and historians of women since have tended to overlook the "sister sailors"– those women whose lives are so vividly evoked by this exhibit.

Nautical enthusiasts in the twentieth century have known better, providing an avid readership for the several popular accounts and published collections of sea-going women's letters and diaries. And these do make fascinating reading: romantic yet somewhat perplexing tales of women who left the familiar domestic setting behind and entered the all-male world of the ship and sea, women who braved loneliness, discomfort, sacrifice, and often great hardship to follow their husbands (or, less frequently, their fathers) to distant and exotic places, all for love or duty or both. Theirs are often dramatic and compelling stories, filled

family ensconced in a private dwelling. Women were now considered by their very nature faithful and loving, pious and chaste, morally strong yet physically weak and properly submissive. They belonged in the Home, it was announced in countless books, magazines, speeches, and sermons. In fact, it was women's duty and most crucial work to imbue the Home with all the virtues absent in the cold, competitive, rough-and-tumble public and male world of work and politics. In the Home, they were to cherish and protect their children, and to nurture, restore, and rescue from temptation their men, who returned worn out or, worse, corrupted by the fray. Wife and mother were women's most important roles.

As a number of historians have recently pointed out, this idealized vision of a

The "sister sailors," especially the deep-sea ones, had perhaps the most in common with the pioneer women heading west. Trekking westward or setting sail, these women left home in order to preserve it – they uprooted themselves in order to keep their nuclear families intact. Like so many of the women braving the Overland Trail, merchant and whaling captains' wives and daughters left behind the familiar domestic surroundings to accompany their husbands and fathers on trips or voyages that the men had decided to make. Also like the pioneer women, the women at sea felt keenly the absence of their community of friends and relatives, the customary female networks that supported women as they bore and raised children, cared for their families and homes. But unlike those heading west, the "sister sailors" set off with little or no adult female companionship, alone on a vessel crewed by men. Small wonder they took such pleasure in meeting other women at sea or abroad.

The coasting women could be considered the more fortunate, because they were rarely gone for long, and because they were more likely to perform an active function onboard ship. As Chapter 1 illustrates, coasting women often served as actual members of the crew, as

Carrie Davis did on her father's small schooner. The coasting sisterhood thus continued the long-standing traditional role for women known as the "helpmeet." In small-scale family enterprises – farming, small shopkeeping, and the like – wives and daughters often pitched in alongside husbands and fathers, even if it meant performing men's work. For centuries, in these sorts of family partnerships, availability of the extra pair of hands often mattered more than rigid ideas about gender-appropriate activities. But, still, women's involvement in such family partnerships stemmed from their relationships to men. Coasting women, so far as we know, rarely joined a crew on their own; they came aboard mainly as wives or daughters.

Deep-water "sister sailors" went to sea because they were wives or daughters, too, but they went less as traditional "helpmeets" than as companions, reflecting newer ideas about the importance of conjugal closeness and emotional ties in the Victorian nuclear family. Again, we're not sure of the total numbers. But we do know of hundreds of merchants and whaling captains who brought to sea their wives and sometimes their children in their attempt to mitigate the loneliness imposed by distance from home and reinforced by rank on board ship. As Chapters 2 and 3 describe, the Rowlands, Joneses, and Clarkes, sailing in the American merchant fleet, and the Roses, Jennings, and Browns on whalers, met up with dozens of their counterparts in ports around the world and even mid-ocean.

Generally only captains were allowed to bring family members, and thus the women served as tangible reminders of the captain's privileges and the personal costs of seafaring for the rest of the men in the crew. Sometimes crew members complained about the women onboard, and some shipowners did not approve of the practice, but it was generally tolerated as the price to pay for a captain's loyalty and career longevity. Since captains' wives did not act as members of

the crew on these larger vessels and longer voyages, the women's contribution to the enterprise was less obvious. These "sister sailors" occasionally helped out by learning to navigate and assisting in determining the ship's position and course, or by keeping the ship's log, or by nursing the ill among the crew. But their main function was to create a Home, that refuge or oasis, for the captain onboard that most unhomelike place, the sailing ship.

The "sister sailors," then, did not flout convention so much as push it to or even beyond its logical limits. The choices they made, or were made for them, underscore how female identity at the time was defined by family position, especially by relationship to men. But in accompanying their men to sea and in attempting to keep their nuclear families intact, these women were forced to leave behind the broader communities of kinship and neighborhood. To be a proper wife meant that they could not always be a good daughter, perhaps caring for aging parents, or a helpful sister, or a close friend. To serve as moral center in their families meant they had to forsake active church membership. To create proper Home meant they had to live, for months or even years, in a tiny space eked out of an aggressively male workplace. Perhaps worst of all, to accompany their husbands meant compromising their ability to bear and raise their children: young children at sea were exposed to all kinds of unaccustomed dangers, and once they reached school age, were commonly left behind with relatives or friends for the sake of their education. Perhaps no other female experience revealed so clearly the potential contradictions between the different roles women were called upon to occupy in Victorian America.

A great irony is that more and more "sister sailors" joined their husbands and fathers onboard ship in the late nineteenth century just as commercial sail and the whale fishery began to decline. Coasting and fishing under sail persisted well into the twentieth century, but the

heyday of America's great, graceful sailing vessels was over by the 1870s or so, eclipsed by steam technology and undercut by foreign competition. From their ambiguous position, marginal to the enterprise yet another important presence in the seagoing community of the ship, the blue-water women illustrate for us how ideas about masculinity, femininity, and family life structured the social relations of nautical work, the hierarchy of rank and skill onboard, and the links stretched thin between seafarers and shore communities.

The Sailor's Magazine, a nineteenth-century evangelical publication aimed at improving both the lot and the morals of seamen, noted in March, 1858 that "most of those among seamen who have families, do not see them oftener than once in two, three or four years... The evils and sad effects of such a course are many and great... We hope the time may come when every married man in this part of the world will be accompanied by his wife. 'What, therefore, God hath joined together, let not man put asunder.'" The following essays, and the exhibit this catalog accompanies, testify to how strongly the Long Island "sister sailors" felt the force of the Biblical injunction, and to how poignantly they tried to accommodate the contradictory demands made on them by their families and their society.

THE MERCHANT WIVES OF NEW YORK:

Long Island Coasting Women

by Mary Anne Wallace

**Schooner at Orient Wharf and Schooner
Artist: William Steeple Davis**
For many generations the farmers of Long Island hamlets sent their produce to market by schooner or sloop. Indeed, it could be said that the waters of Long Island Sound were whitened by their sails, particularly in the harvesting season. In September 1850 an observer at the eastern extremity of the peninsula of Orient counted "sixty-four sailing vessels, sloops, schooners, and coasters" within view.

When we think about the days of sail, we tend to picture vessels such as merchant clippers, whalers, and even passenger packets. We rarely remember the coasters, the craft that carried mundane cargoes along the eastern seaboard and to and from the West Indies. They lacked glamour, perhaps, but were nevertheless important.

Unlike the merchant ships and whalers with their ocean-crossing voyages, the coasters, as their name indicates, stayed closer to the land. Generally rigged as single-masted sloops or multi-masted schooners, with fore-and-aft sails for maneuverability and to permit them to be operated with small crews, these vessels

varied greatly in size and hull form. The smallest "bay coasters" could be as small as 12 tons and 50 feet in length. By the beginning of the twentieth century the largest coal schooners were among the largest sailing vessels afloat, measuring 3,000 tons and about 300 feet in length, and having six (and in some cases seven) masts.

Whether they stayed within Long Island Sound, plied the bays of New England, worked the estuaries of Chesapeake Bay, or sailed to New Orleans or the West Indies, the windborne sloops and schooners formed an important aspect of the maritime industry. To quote the nautical historian Charles S. Morgan, they were "the errand boys" of the nineteenth and early twentieth centuries. Although steamboats and railroads had claimed most of the valuable coastal freight and passengers by the middle of the nineteenth century, wind-powered coasters continued to lug bulk cargoes from port to port and section to section into the 1930s. For the most part they carried necessary but prosaic cargoes such as cotton, coal, ice, lumber, bricks, clay, stone, lime, and salt. On Long Island Sound, farm produce was an important freight. The large number of sugar refineries located in the Greenpoint section of Brooklyn in the nineteenth century indicates that another agricultural product, cane sugar, was a significant cargo.

Whether the consignment was clay or cabbages, coasting remained profitable well into the twentieth century. Coal became an important cargo in the 1870s as railroad lines expanded, mills changed from water power to steam power to electricity, and trolley cars and electric lights were introduced to more communities.

Long Island bricks, Maine lumber and granite came into demand as east coast cities expanded. The *Village Queen* of Stony Brook, with Captain William Lester Hawkins wife Mary Ann, and their children on board, carried most of the freestone and granite for the east wing of the Capitol and Washington Monument, until stopped by the Civil

War, but not before the entire Hawkins family had witnessed the battle of the ironclad warships *Merrimac* and the *Monitor* from the deck of their ship on March 9, 1862. In the twentieth century, Florida's land boom added to the continuing need for schooners which were an economical way to transport building materials south. Another 1920s event, Prohibition, provided an illegal cargo for schooners involved in rum running.

The lack of good roads allowed northern New England schooner captains to play the part of oceangoing truck drivers right up until the 1930s, long after many areas to the south had seen the end of coasting. A last – and dramatic – need for their craft came about in 1942 when Nelson Rockefeller, the director of the Inter-American Affairs Bureau, made a request for 300 schooners in an attempt to out-maneuver German submarines that were blockading the eastern seaboard.

Although coasters differed from whalers and merchant ships in the routes they sailed and the cargoes they carried, they shared a number of characteristics. Business matters, storms, and risks of accident and ill health were much the same whether one was on a merchant ship, a whaler, or a coaster. Many coasting captains also took their wives and families to sea with them. Little attention had been devoted to the history of coasters, but even less notice has been paid to the women who sailed aboard of them. One finds only the briefest mention in just a few maritime histories. The lack of published sources can be attributed, in part, to the small number of coaster women's diaries and letters in our historical societies and museums. Possibly many are still hidden in attics waiting for some perceptive family member to find them and donate them to a public institution. It could be the case, however, that family and friends who received letters were not inclined to save them, as most were sent from ports with familiar names such as New York, Baltimore, Portland, Boston, and New Orleans, rather than from the distant, foreign ports where most merchant and whaler mail was posted.

Fortunately, a few documents have survived to provide us with the means of learning what women experienced aboard the unglamorous but efficient east coast sloops and schooners. Three are the diaries and letters of three Long Island women – Mary Rowland, who sailed on the schooner *Stephen H. Townsend*, and the brigs *Thomas W. Rowland* and *Mary E. Rowland* for two decades beginning 1852; Carrie Hubbard Davis, who sailed on the Long Island Sound schooner *Jacob S. Ellis* in the 1870s; and Ettabel Raynor, who accompanied her father on a coasting voyage to Florida on the 620-ton schooner *Ruth B. Cobb* in 1915 – which allow us a rare and valuable insight into the lives of the sister coaster women.

Mary Rowland, like a number of women whose husbands went wherever they could find a cargo, sailed on both merchant and coasting voyages. Of spe-

Carrie Davis
In 1873 Carrie Hubbard married coasterman Charlie Davis, and thereafter sailed with him on the schooner *Jacob S. Ellis*, the third member of a three-person crew.

Mary Rowland
Mary, wife of Captain Henry Rowland, first sailed as a twenty-year-old bride in 1852, at the start of a seafaring career that spanned 24 years.

Cargo Deck of *Ruth B. Cobb*
With decks piled high with produce, coal, or lumber, as well as with holds filled with cargo, coasters were the delivery trucks of their day.

cial interest are her letters to her sister and children written during her coasting existence in the 1870s. Carrie Davis sailed in that decade too, though her experiences were in sharp contrast to Mary Rowland's, for not only was her voyaging confined to Long Island Sound, but her maritime life was more active than Mary's, as she was the third person in a three-person crew. Then, with Ettabel Raynor's 1915 diary, we leave the Victorian world of Mary Rowland and Carrie Davis, and move into the modern world of a twentieth-century single young woman.

children convey similar thoughts about her relationship with her husband. In a lengthy sea letter to "Sister Hannah," begun on January 1, 1873, Mary wrote, "where the Treasure is there will the Heart be yet my mind cannot be at rest in one respect for on the land are my Children that need a Mother's constant care and in the Sea and often thousands of miles from home is my Husband toiling for us all and whose constant wish is for me to go with him so I divide my time with them and do the best I can for them all." Then, later in the same letter, she revealed that Henry shared her feelings, confiding, "We heartily wish that H. had some other business this is so much care and constant exposure to danger and sickness. And unless I can go sometimes we must be separated most all the time with the exception of one month or six weeks out of the year and that is unhappiness to us both."

The many sea voyages she made were, indeed, a sign of her wifely devotion, for by going on voyage Mary became doubly subject to Henry's domination, because at sea he was captain of the ship in addition to his natural role of head of the family. Even if she wanted to, Mary could make no attempt to influence his decisions at sea, writing in February 1870, "I often stand in the door and watch... preparations for a squall with nervous excitement and feel as if the work could not be done quick enough and if I must request all to be in haste but I never say anything to worry anyone."

However, she refused to accept outright commands. In her January 1, 1873, letter to Hannah, she revealed this, saying, "Men in general are not overstocked with patience and on shipboard he [Henry] is used to command and I have occasionaly hinted that my name is not on his Ship's Articles [even] if I did promise to love and obey him some 20 years ago when I engaged to be his Mate for life... I really love to do his pleasure but revolt at the sound of a command from him to me and if he not thinking speaks thus to me I am quite apt to resent it instead of overlooking it."

Woodhull, Mary Emma, and Henrietta Rowland

Mary Rowland raised a family of four on board, giving birth to one - Woodhull - at sea. Her husband Henry ordered the American flag run up so that his son was born an American citizen, though he was two years old before he set foot on his native soil.

Wave breaking over the decks of the *Ruth B. Cobb*

The only alternative to long separations from a mariner husband was a life at sea, even attended as it was with inevitable discomforts and dangers.

Mary Rowland first went to sea as a bride. At the time she wrote the coasting letters, however, she was in her late thirties, and her three children, Mary Emma, Henrietta ("Etta"), and Woodhull, had been left at home in Setauket. While she deeply regretted having to leave her family behind, Mary, like many other maritime wives, gave first importance to her role as wife. In a February 10, 1870, letter to her sister Hannah she expressed this, writing:

Were it not for [Henry] I'd never go to sea but it is his business and after having been as much as I have and then stay[ed] home without his company I sometimes feel allmost like "the eagle caged" and then I have so many pressing invitations to go a voyage that it is hard to refuse especially if your heart is allways here as mine ever is so off I come to share his fate and divide my time with him and the children. It is hard to be separated from either. There is continually a void in your heart that a True Wife and mother only knows.

Several other letters to her sister and her

Despite this complaint it is evident that Mary really did "love to do his pleasure," for she never overcame her dread of stormy weather, and feared that each gale could be the one to end their lives. As she described in her 1870 letter to her sister, "we have experienced a most terrific Gale...

The Brig was run before it as long as it was thought prudent that we might get well clear of the Coast It is a bad place off Hatteras in winter time shoals being a long distance from the main land And we were obliged to lay too for 56 hours while the Gale was at its height having the Brig under the least possible Sail And thus far thank God we have been kept in Safety our little Brig riding the great Seas like a Gull I often think which is going to last the longest the Gale or the Vessel... I can never get accustomed to [storms] enough to not suffer fear during these times when all the elements are at war. The loud roaring of the great waves, the lightning flash and Thunder's roar are not pleasant company. The tempestuous sea seems trying to swallow us up or rather down I should say. And then O don't the Sharks have a glorious feast. Sometimes I wonder if they do not have an idea of what is going on above them and so get the great Whales and Mermaids to assist them to set the waves in commotion.

Mary Rowland's attitude toward mail was less straightforward, being the ambivalent mixture of delight and dread that was common with the seafaring wives. Thus, Mary's comment to her sister Hannah, that "I am allways very anxious to get [letters] and then I am quite nervous about reading them," penned on March 4, 1870, was similar to statements made by numerous nineteenth-century women who were far from home. Whether a woman was away from home for a year, a month, a week, or even a few days, her eagerness to get mail was tinged by a fear the letters might contain news of family illness or death. When Mary was in New Orleans in January 1873, she wrote to Hannah that she and Henry had received two letters "from home which I was most anxious to get yet allways feel afraid to open them for fear I may read unpleasant news that the children are sick or something wrong." The great distance from their families often meant that women like Mary waited weeks or sometimes months for information about the outcome of a family crisis.

Carrie Davis, her husband, her father, and her journal
Carrie Davis accompanied her husband Charlie and her father Captain William Hubbard on Long Island Sound voyages from Orient to Connecticut and back, using her journal to record among other things, the vast amounts of food she cooked on the small galley stove.

Carrie Davis was one of the few coaster wives who did not have to wait long for news. As she sailed between Orient, Long Island, and Connecticut towns on the north shore of Long Island Sound, she was never far, in either time or distance, from her mother at home. Nevertheless, both women wrote almost daily to each other, so that Carrie was in constant touch with the domestic circle of Orient. Consequently, the rich fund of Hubbard-Davis manuscript material held by the William Steeple Davis Trust includes much correspondence as well as Carrie's diaries.

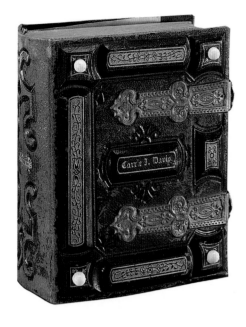

In the late 1870s, Carrie, her husband Charlie, and her father, Captain William Hubbard, were the three-person crew aboard the *Jacob S. Ellis*. The *Ellis*, with its varied vegetable cargoes which were carried from local farms anywhere within the bounds of Long Island Sound where there might be a market, was similar to what was called, in northern New England, a "bay" schooner. As described by Ernest Dodge, bay schooners took a "cargo wherever it could be found, and carried anything anywhere on the coast for anybody."

In contrast to Mary Rowland, who had no role other than companion and wife to her husband Henry on board his much larger vessels, Carrie was an active member of the three-person crew of the little *Ellis*, assuming the responsibilities of both cook and steward as she shopped, cooked, served meals, and attended to all matters in the cabin, in effect carrying out exactly the same tasks as she did at home, so that at times when perusing her diary it is hard to tell whether she was on shore or in the swaying and

Carrie Davis album

Life on the *Jacob S. Ellis*, encapsulated in the family photograph album, was a family affair, for Carrie's mother Jane Hubbard, the village midwife, often accompanied them to Norwich, Connecticut, and friends and neighbors were often encountered in port.

sometimes stormy environment of a schooner. On Wednesday March 13, 1878, Carrie noted, "we came to Norwich – had a good run, wind and tide being favorable," and added: "During the week I have done considerable cooking &c, baked two pans of sweet Indian meal bread, a pan of sugar cake and two pans of nice wheat bread.

Today cooked steak and potatoes for breakfast, knead bread, made Oyster pie for dinner, made a doz[en] stickies, thirteen sugar cookies, two pans of wheat bread, a pan of biscuit and two pans of sweet meal bread, prepared nearly a lb. of suet for shortening, boiled some sauce [pickle] for tomorrow, besides other work. Eve., Charlie & I took a walk up st[reet] – He has been quite busy through the week, helping attend to the produce aboard &c. –

Carrie's active role, although unusual, was not totally unknown. In December 1883, the crew of the station Rye, New Hampshire, U. S. Life-Saving Service reached the distressed Maine schooner *Rockaway* and found only three people aboard: Captain Kingsbury, his wife, and their fifteen-year-old son. Although we do not know Mrs. Kingsbury's role aboard, we do know that captains' wives on trading coasters – floating general stores – were actively involved in selling merchandise to customers in isolated northern New England coastal towns. Often, as an account of the trade on the Penobscot River points out, the wife was more effective in selling than the husband and "seemed, even more than he, to realize the value of small talk with male and especially female customers." Carrie Hubbard Davis was certainly interested in the disposal of the cargo, and sent daily letters to her mother reporting on the state of the market: "The Turnips and Onions go dull..." she wrote on December 19, 1877. "Are expecting to go down the River tomorrow morning if there's a chance – will probably stop at New London awhile... but of course a good deal depends upon the market and weather." If Carrie had been even more directly involved in the sale, one wonders, might the captain of the *Jacob S. Ellis* have found better markets for his produce?

Even though the *Ellis* sailed back and forth within the limits of Long Island Sound and not across the Pacific or Atlantic Oceans, Carrie was as eager to see the sights in unfamiliar ports as her sister sailors on larger vessels. After the day's business, she and Charlie explored the local shops and parks, and visited aboard other schooners. A diary entry dated June 14, 1878, and penned in Norwich, Connecticut, reported, "In the evening Charlie and I called aboard the Odd Fellow. Capt. [Lorenzo] Dyer had his wife and their younger children along with him on the vessel." A Fourth of July jaunt was described in a July 8, 1879, letter to her mother. "Dear Ma," she wrote:

I thought I would write you a few lines. We arrived in Orient Saturday. Left Norwich that day about two p.m. and reached the wharf at Orient at half past seven p.m. Had it quite rough after getting into the sound, as the wind was strong, and the tide ahead.

I wrote you a letter the day we arrived at Norwich, which was late on Wednesday, had rather a dull run you see. It was so calm Tuesday, we didn't pass by Plum Island till afternoon ...

There was considerable noise at Norwich, ringing of bells & firing of guns early a.m., and at noon – The blowing of horns and use of powder began over night—

Two steamers went from there with excursions, each having a brass band so we heard some good music. The weather was very warm indeed but we managed to get along with some degree of comfort – We regaled ourselves at times with iced lemonade, cake and Brazil nuts – We brought some nuts and lemons home for you, in case you had not gone, so you see you were not forgotten—

In the p.m. Charlie & I went up the stream in the sharpy, passed under several bridges, and had quite a pleasant row – Talked of going to the park, but it was too warm to make much of an effort, and towards night a heavy shower set in. – Pa expects to load soon– but when you write next direct to Orient – The market was dull last trip, but he hopes the produce will give better satisfaction next time—

These activities (if not the preoccupation with produce and markets) compare with those of a fifteen-year-old Orient girl, Nancy Latham, who spent seven weeks aboard a family friend's schooner in the year 1900. In her reminiscent account, *My Trip on the Water*, Nancy related that she and the Potter family (also of Orient) spent July Fourth in Camden, New Jersey, where, "We went to Washington Park which is just below Gloucester, where we had a fine time on the shoots, toboggan slides, the ferris wheel and merry-go-round.

Another time we went there at night. The park looked just lovely with all of the colored electric lights and also the ferris wheel which could be seen at a long distance. Then we saw the electric fountain which was too beautiful to be described...

One day went to Willow Grove about eight miles out of the city. We passed John Wanamaker's summer residence and many other handsome cottages.

We went to Fairmont Park through which the Schuylkill River runs, where the Centennial was held twenty four years ago. There we saw all of the animals.

We went to Independence Hall and saw the old Liberty Bell and other relics.

Although Nancy made no reference to church-going, Carrie, Mary Rowland, and Ettabel Raynor all followed another custom that was common to other maritime women and their families when they were anchored at some port, that of honoring the Sabbath. Away from home on a Sunday, Carrie and Charlie Davis often attended more than one service or prayer meeting, such as on December 29, 1878, when they "attended the Central Methodist Church in the morning – a Cong. Church in the p.m., and the Broadway Church in the evening."

Charlie Davis, scrapbook
When cargoes had been unloaded the evenings on the schooner became tranquil, and Carrie's husband Charlie Davis busied himself with his hobbies, such as binding albums for Carrie's collections of cards.

"Well, here we are in Fernandina," wrote Ettabel Raynor from Florida in February, 1915.

It is a pretty place and I guess I'll have a pretty good time here, but too short for Dad says we won't be here much longer than a week. I am disappointed in that, for a week is a mighty short time in which to visit a place... I didn't go to church this morning, as I knew no-one, and felt rather strange about going here alone... [In the evening] I wanted to go to church, so Dad and I left about half-past seven. I went to the Methodist Church, and though the service seemed like home, I was just a little disappointed, for not one person spoke to me, and I couldn't help but think of the cordiality of Trinity which would be exchanged at home. The service commenced at 7:30 P.M., and closed at 8:30 P.M., and this seemed mighty strange to me.

By the early 1880s, both Carrie Davis and Mary Rowland had made their last coasting voyages, and Long Island whaling was finished. Coasters, however, continued their voyages for another fifty years. Ettabel Raynor's diary records her experiences from January 20 to March 1, 1915, on a round trip from New York to Florida aboard her father's schooner *Ruth B. Cobb* when she was twenty years old. She inhabited a shore world that was greatly changed from the Victorian one in which Carrie Davis and Mary Rowland lived. Women's hair was less elaborately styled; clothing was shorter and simpler. Girls also had more educational and employment opportunities. While Ettabel, like Carrie and Mary, toured local attractions, she was able to see the sights from a bicycle, a car, and a motorized launch. On February 8 she recorded one such busy day.

After we had finished dinner, Mrs. Flynn, Mrs. Cole [young wives from other schooners in port] and I jumped in the boat, and we all came aboard here. At two o'clock we took to the automobile which stood at the end of the boardwalk and had a nice long drive. We drove to the beach first... Then we came back through Fernandina, then went to a place called Amelia City. It is a very small place indeed, but awfully pretty. It is right on the bluff, and has splendid building sites. The houses are well kept up, and altogether it is a beautiful little spot. On our way there we drove through a regular grove of moss covered trees, and it certainly made a picture. I should love to have had a camera...

Raynor family snapshots and the *Ruth B. Cobb*
Artist: T.W. Willis

Larger schooners like the *Ruth B. Cobb*, with their bigger crews, meant that skippers like Captain Eugene Raynor could enjoy taking their daughters on coasting voyages to the exotic ports of New Orleans and Florida in conditions of relative comfort.

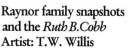

Unsurprisingly, Ettabel noted next day that "There is so much to do all the time that I find it hard to keep my journal written up." Her sea world was very much like Mary Rowland's, however, for Ettabel had no role to play on the coaster apart from providing companionship for the captain, her father. Other than one mention of being at the helm as the *Cobb* was towed into Fernandina, and making a fly for the schooner, Ettabel filled in her time by embroidering, reading, learning to recognize foreign flags, and writing in her diary.

Even youthful, mundane diaries such as Ettabel's provide us with invaluable insights into the twilight of coasting under sail. We learn about the hazards, as well. Two of the major hazards to navigation were steamers and wrecks, simply because the coasters sailed across the congested steamer lanes south of New York. It was not at all uncommon for steamers to sink schooners. Both Ettabel and Mary Rowland noted how uncomfortably close steamers came: In a letter penned in January 1873, Mary described lying to in a snow squall off New Haven Harbor, saying, "The steam boats passed very near to us, in fact, we found ourselves anchored directly in their track as they went to and from [New York] City and I feared we might get run into but our light was kept brightly burning in the fore rigging."

The danger did not lessen in the twentieth century. On January 29, 1915, Ettabel recorded, "A schooner struck a steamer broadside, and the two of them sank in ten minutes." On their return trip, she noted that only daylight and her father's sharp eyesight and knowledge of the sea prevented the *Cobb* from running afoul of the sunken steamer. "We were all right for we could see it, but on a dark night, it might mean the loss of many lives."

Nancy Latham described a firsthand experience of a collision at sea in her memoir:

Thursday morning about seven thirty, we heard a great crash, men running, and lots of noise. Gert and I got out of bed and looked out and saw two masts sticking up the bow. When Capt. Potter came down he said that it was very foggy and that a barkentine had tried to cross our bows and we had struck her amidships and knocked a great hole in her. Then the wreck had drifted away in the fog and they couldn't see her. It had not damaged our boat much. The fore top mast was gone and some thing else that made her leak.

Fortunately, Ettabel, Carrie, Mary, and the great majority of maritime wives did not experience the disasters that befell some of their sister sailors. There were still seasickness, accident, and illness to be feared, however, and Mary Rowland was often lonely for her children and kin. As the farthest ranging coasterwoman, she yearned for and at the same time feared news from home. And, like hundreds of other seafaring women, she wrote long sea letters and journals as a way of passing the long, lonely hours at

sea. And, whether valued and deliberately saved by their families or just forgotten in dusty attics, the sea letters and diaries penned by the sister sailors now provide us with an unrivaled insight into the female world of coasting that ceased to exist sixty years ago.

Raynor Family snap shots
Voyaging on the bigger schooners offered adventure and fun for daughters like Ettabel Raynor, who could play with ship's pets and even occasionally take over the helm.

THE MERCHANT WIVES OF NEW YORK:

Blue-Water Merchant Wives

by Joan Druett

The magnitude of the coasting fleet of the eastern seaboard of America can be easily ascertained just by glancing through the pages of any nineteenth-century ships' register, for the pages are overwhelmingly dominated by the names and numbers of a multitude of sloops, schooners and brigs. There were

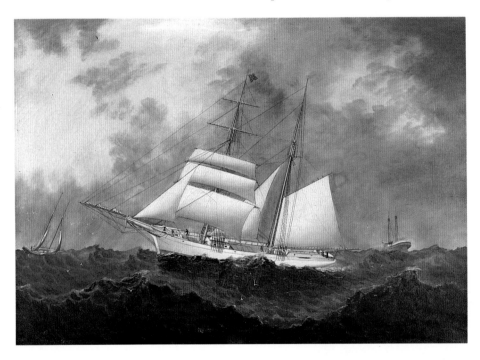

The Atalanta
Artist: William York
Martha Maria Bayles sailed on the merchant bark *Atalanta* in the 1880s.

so many of these fore-and-aft rigged craft in the crowded New England ports, that it was often hard to tell one from the other. However, they did vary greatly in size and tonnage, and so there was a definite hierarchy.

This implies, of course, that the conditions for the merchant wives varied greatly too. Carrie Davis did not describe the accommodations on the *Jacob S. Ellis*, but hinted at much in her lists of work

accomplished, such as painting the cabin, making and hanging curtains, sewing quilts for the berths, and braiding a mat for the floor. There was just one day-cabin, where she, her husband, and her father took their meals at a narrow table with seat-topped lockers on either side; the berths would have been narrow wooden bunks, also built over lockers, each with a lip to stop the mattress from sliding out, and a curtain for privacy. The decks of the schooner were equally cramped, for Captain Hubbard used up every available inch when stowing cargo, carrying heavy deckloads of hay, lumber, and rails, as well as filling his hold with produce such as turnips, carrots, and potatoes.

Carrie Davis did describe the accommodations on a schooner that was destined to sail on much more extensive voyages than Captain Hubbard could ever have planned. "Capt. Charles Franklin arrived in Orient [March] 29th with a handsome 3 master schooner which he has lately had built at Kenebunk Maine," she wrote to her grandfather Culver of Southampton, in April, 1873.

While the Sch. lay at the Wharf in Orient it was thronged with visitors, I was among the number that went aboard. It is very large & beautifully furnished. The cabin floor is covered with brussels carpet, and contains a pretty lounge, a black walnut extension table, chairs etc. etc. The Captain's room is like an elegant furnished parlor, it is carpeted with brussels, contains a beautiful cabinet organ & book case, & handsome stuffed chairs fancy lamp & rich curtains, pictures & other ornaments. The ceiling has gilt moldings. The sleeping accomodations are very nice. The rooms belonging to the mates & steward are also good. The kitchen & pantry are very convenient, and the whole affair is pronounced most beautiful.

This description was of the *J.J. Moore*, a splendid vessel of 411 tons that was probably rather similar to Captain Eugene Raynor's 620-ton schooner *Ruth B. Cobb*. Other Long Island coasterwomen – Maria Cartwright Baldwin on the *Adelia Felicia*, Mary Lurch Bayles on the *Lavinia Belle*, Harriet Aldrich Thompson on the *Addie P. Avery*, and Mary Satterly Rowland on the *Stephen*

H. Townsend – voyaged on schooners that were somewhat less luxurious than the *J.J. Moore*, most being rated at something less than two hundred tons. Their waterborne homes were often unstable, and the furnishings flew about rather readily. As Mary Rowland wryly commented in January 1873, going to sea could "prove a lucrative business for a person whose occupation was mending broken furniture." Like Mary, too, many of the coasting wives found that bed was "the only dry place." Nevertheless, they travelled in a great deal more comfort than Carrie Davis could ever have expected – and because of this, they traveled farther, too. It was a relatively simple matter for the skipper of a 200-ton coasting schooner or square-rigged brig or bark to extend his voyage to South America or the far side of the Atlantic in a hunt for markets there, something which Captain Hubbard could never have possibly contemplated in the tiny 12-ton *Ellis*.

Captain Henry Rowland was one of those who broadened his range to include blue-water voyaging, so that his wife's career at sea is worth detailed study, for it indicates so vividly her transition from coasting wife to adventurer in the deep-water trades. Mary Satterly Rowland sailed first as a bride, in the fall of 1852: "In the schooner Stephen H. Townsend," she wrote, in a later memorandum of her seafaring life.

I sailed from New York to Havanna from thence to Boston, from Boston to Bridgeport, Conn., from thence to N.Y. [then] I went to L[ong] I[sland] and remained till Oct. 1853 [when I] sailed from New York to Sierra Leone, West Coast of Africa, in the winter of 1854 bringing back to N. Y. a Cargo of Dry hides and Peanuts In the Spring [of] 1854 [I sailed] From N. Y. to Terragona in Spain carrying out a full cargo of stones and bringing back to N. Y. wine Almonds & figs, in June I remained in L.I. till Oct. then went to N. Y., Etta was a young babe.

In Brig Thomas W. Rowland Sailed from N.Y. in 1855 to Buenas Ayres with a cargo of Flour. From thence sailed with a Cargo of Salted hides for Antwerp ... Then Sailed for Genoa with a cargo of Sugar from thence proceeded down the Mediterranean seeking freight and went to Malaga, Spain. There loaded the Brig with Lemons Raisins Wine & Figs and sailed for New Orleans. 1856, At New Orleans took onboard a Cargo of flour and sailed for Rio Janeiro from thence returned to New Orleans with a Cargo of Coffee in 1857 Sailed from N.Y with a Cargo of Cotton to Marseilles, France... and went down to Malaga and loaded the Brig with Wine Raisins & figs and went to New Orleans. from N.O. went to Genoa with a Cargo of Cotton.

In 1858 ... proceeded to Palermo, Sicily, There took on a cargo of Oranges and Lemons and proceeded to Philadelphia. And from thence to N.York... 1859 Sailed from N.Y. with a Cargo of Merchandize to Mobile, Alabama... there loaded with lumber and went to Rio Janeiro, At Rio Janeiro loaded with Coffee and went to New Orleans, from N.O. went to N.Y. and the Brig went to France. I remained on Long Island untill Aug. 1860 Then I went to Boston and joined my Husband there from thence we sailed to Philadelphia. There loaded lumber to Buenas Ayres. From Buenas Ayres went to Rio Janeiro... after remaining in that port 2 months

being detained for a cargo... took in a Cargo of Coffee and went to Malta... At Marseilles we loaded Wine and went to Rio Janeiro Expecting to obtain a Cargo of Coffee to the U.S., but the War was then raging between the North and South and Merchants dared not ship their property fearing it might fall into the hands of the privateers that had begun their devastations on Vessels bound into or owned in Northern Ports and the southern Ports were many of them under a blockade... so we were obliged to go the long distance in ballast to N.Y....

Detail of *Atalanta*
Artist: William York
While the decks of large vessels like the *Atalanta* were spacious, the captain's wife was confined by propriety to promenading the quarter deck.

In March 1862 my Husband bought a part of the Bark Glenwood having previous[ly] sold his part of the Brig. The Glenwood was chartered to [the] Government to take supplies of fire wood to the Army South and we sailed for Santa Rosa Island in Pensacola bay and there discharged a part of the freight while lying at Santa Rosa Island and the remainder took by Pensacola City after the evacuation of the rebel troops.

Mary Rowland's experience is representative of the varied cargoes and routes that made up American maritime commerce in the mid-nineteenth century. The large and elegant packet ships that made scheduled runs across the North Atlantic were but the most publicized of the merchant ships great and small that carried raw materials from the Americas to European ports and returned with manufactured goods and emigrants. In the Pacific, the trade with China increased after the opium wars of the 1840s, and the California gold rush of 1848-50 brought a flood of ships west and an ongoing trade between the East Coast and California round Cape Horn. Other ships carried goods and produce between North and South America, or made the run round the Cape of Good Hope to India. A large vessel of the 1830s was 700 tons and perhaps 150 feet long; by the 1850s the celebrated clipper ships were around 1,500 tons and 220 feet long; and the large post-Civil War deep-water sailing ships approached 2,500 tons and 275 feet in length.

Captain and Mrs. E. Gates-James aboard the *Lynton,* **1905**
Captain and Family inside Cabin
Artist: Ron Druett.
Below decks, the captain's wife and family were limited to the after cabins. On merchant ships the saloon could be quite grand, but the transom cabin of a whaling ship (about six feet by eight in size) was a cramped place for a family to live.

In a commercial world emphasizing "tramp" ships that carried whatever cargoes were available wherever they were destined, flexibility was essential when searching out freights and markets. As the turn of the century progressed, investment in bigger vessels became economically advantageous, as bigger or more varied cargoes could be carried. Those cargoes could prove strangely hazardous, as Mary Satterly Rowland found when the freight of dried figs and raisins her husband picked up in Malaga, Spain, in September 1856, began to ripen and produce gruesome livestock in the doldrums on the way to New Orleans. "Thermometer stands on 91 down in the Cabin," she wrote on October 6, "but the steam that arises from the cargo makes it much warmer than it otherwise would be...

"And we are tormented with vermin, more so than ever before, roaches come by thousands... and it is impossible to scald them, they move so quick. The flies have nearly all left us as we get further out at sea, but we have some more troublesome visitors of late, Musketoes have taken up their abode on board by dozens and whence they came I know not, they must be a tribe of Ocean wanderers. Oh dear how they bite... And now besides these plagues we have still other ones on board, white crawling worms about an inch long come out of the cargo of figs and raisins and large numbers make their appearance in the Cabin and more particularly in my room. They keep hid during the day time and like the Cockroaches & musketoes make their Debut at night, they crawl up on the ceiling overhead and then fall down in a short time but Oh dear they like to hide in my mattress best of all places and although I watch for and destroy all that I can find before I retire, often I am awakened during the night by them as they drop down upon me and then commence to crawl over me occasionaly taking a nip as their appetites suits them."

The bigger the merchant vessels were, the more comfortable they became, so that in oceangoing square-rigged ships like the 1,136-ton bark *Emma T. Crowell*, which sailed out of New York to Asia in the 1880s, the quarters could be quite magnificent. Fred Essex, who took passage in the *Emma* from Shanghai to New York, wrote that she was "a very comfortably fitted up ship.

In the house aft and surrounded by a spacious poop deck, there was the dining cabin and a large parlor saloon, fixed up with plush covered lounges, nice easy chairs, the sides veneered with stained walnut and maple and fixed to one end a nice little "Bord" pianette. Luxury this, a piano on board ship. Of course the piano stool, when I learnt to balance myself on it properly, was my little throne. In the evening the captain [Andrew Pendleton] and family would assemble and I would go through a light repertory suited to the occasion. A stirring fantasia representing the "Battle of Bunker Hill" was in most request and my piece de resistance. It did not require the amount of execution of a Chopin mazurka, but it brought down the house.

Even the relatively small 500-ton merchant bark *Mary & Louisa*, which Mary Swift Jones of Setauket boarded as a

Women Hanging Laundry on Shipboard, 1911
Seaman Doing Laundry on the *Ruth B. Cobb*
While the steward might be paid to do washing, it was more common for wives to do laundry for herself, the Captain and their children aboard. - a hard task on a rolling ship, with a scarcity of fresh water and no guarantee that the clothes would dry. Crew members were responsible for their own washing.

twenty-four-year-old bride in 1858, boasted beautiful after quarters, albeit on a smaller scale. Freeman Pulsifer, who sailed from Hong Kong to Shanghai as a passenger in May, 1860, noted in his journal that the "accommodations are fine and we have a very excellent table." Mary's cabin boy, Egbert Bull Smith, who published a colorful account of the voyage much later, described the "forward" cabin – the dining room of the ship where that excellent fare was served – in detail. The table was set directly under the large skylight, which let in sunlight from the deck above, and behind it "a large mirror was secured and a beautiful swinging lamp hung over the table. This cabin," Smith went on, "was painted pure white, with two gilded mouldings around the top. In the starboard after corner, eight rifles, with bayonets nicely polished, stood in a rack."

The rifles served for more than decora-

tion, as Freeman Pulsifer testified on May 17, 1860, when the vessel was becalmed near the "Chusan" islands, "a well known resort of pirates... Hands been rubbing up the muskets and we have been amusing ourselves in shooting at bottles." The target practice proved unnecessary, though the danger was real. According to Egbert Bull Smith, the bark was attacked by pirates earlier in the voyage, as the *Mary & Louisa* negotiated the Malacca Straits in the South China Sea. The crew fended off the raiders with double charges of buckshot, revolvers, and hand grenades, and so the bark escaped.

Less lucky was the 1,647-ton full-rigged ship *Frank N. Thayer*, one of the vessels owned by the Howell family of Quogue. On the 1885 voyage she was commanded by Captain Robert K. "Sunrise" Clarke, who habitually carried his wife and daughter Carrie, aged five at the time. They sailed for New York

Captain Henry Luke Rowland
Storms, fire, and collision were real hazards, but captains like Henry Rowland had the compelling reason of loneliness to ask their wives to share their risky lives at sea.

Bark *Grace Harwar* in a storm
Artist: Ron Druett

from Manila just before Christmas with a cargo of hemp and tar, and with a few Malays in the crew who had been hired as replacements for sick seamen left in port. The Malays became unhappy, on account of some rather summary medical care handed out by the captain (along with a kick) to one of their group who imagined himself mortally ill, and so seized the ship one midnight in January, in the course of a particularly bloody mutiny.

First the helmsman's throat was cut with a hand-made lance, and when Captain Clarke came rushing up the companionway he was slashed across the ribs. Mrs. Clarke flew to her husband's protection, grabbing the native's arm before he could thrust again. "But by that time all hell was loose on the ship," reminisced one of the survivors, Andy Harris of Quogue, to a writer from the *Long Island Forum*. Not only had the regular seamen retreated in disarray to the fo'c'sle and the rigging, completely demoralized by the murder of the first and second mates, but the cargo had been set on fire.

The ship was doomed, so the largest boat was hastily launched while Mrs. Clarke held off the Malays with pistol fire. Then at last they pulled away, with the captain, his family, and the original crewmen aboard, several of them injured. According to a dramatic New York *World-Telegram* account of the incident (published years later, in May 1934), Captain Clarke was so severely wounded that his left lung protruded six inches through the hole the lance had cut in his ribs. His wife managed to push the slippery organ back inside and bind the terrible gash with strips of cloth which she sewed tightly in place. Clarke did recover, "but only because of his good wife's constant care," Harris claimed. And the little girl? She had remained silent and still throughout the dreadful struggle on board the ship, and was equally quiet during the 200-mile escape to the Island of St. Helena. But then, "Carrie was a well behaved child the

whole time," the captain's wife was reported as remarking, in what must be a masterpiece of understatement.

The same New York *World-Telegram* series, published under the title "Women Against the Sea," described another mutiny, but one with a happier ending. The heroine of this tale was Emily Van Dercook Brown, whose statue is now in the Metropolitan Museum of Art. Emily first met Captain John Alexander Brown in Brooklyn, where he was courting her aunt, and married him herself, in 1876 when she was only sixteen. Then the young bride sailed with him in the 736-ton ship *John Harvey*, bound for Peru.

Within days she found that the handsome, stalwart, experienced mariner she had married was a hardcase master, ever-ready with his boots and fists and very prone to confine men in iron shackles. Throughout the first weeks of passage she tried to make up for Brown's brutality, stealing his cigars to give to the men, and making soup for an English sailor, "Black Tom," and surreptitiously feeding it to him when he was in irons. She could not prevent the brewing mutiny, but she did manage to save her husband's life: when the sailors had Captain Brown all trussed up and were set to swing him overboard, she stepped forward, touched Black Tom on the shoulder, and said very clearly, "Gentlemen, please!"

So, while the big merchant vessels were much more luxurious than the plodding coasters – or whaleships, for that matter -- life on board of them was no less hazardous. For any woman who went to sea, storms were a very predictable danger, and Egbert Bull Smith described several impressive squalls and gales in his published account of the voyage of the *Mary & Louisa*. Those who lived on the lee shores of Long Island were certainly aware of the damage storms could do to vessels. When the 596-ton schooner *Nahum Chapin* was driven ashore just east of Quogue on January 21, 1897, watchers on the storm-lashed beach could discern the figures of Captain Eugene Lavey, his wife, child, and the crew of eight men clinging to the foremast rigging and jibboom, but nothing could be done to save them. Similarly, both Mrs. Burtow of Port Jefferson and her husband drowned when the schooner *Jennie Rosaline*, 348 tons, was lost in 1889. Harriet Aldrich Thompson, who sailed often with her husband Captain James Henry Thompson on the schooner *Addie P. Avery*, fortunately did not accompany him on his last voyage in 1878, when the ship struck shoals off Cape Cod and sank, drowning both James and his brother Andrew.

There were plenty of other hazards to be dreaded by the merchant wives. Unmentioned by Mary Rowland, in the last part of her terse accounting of her sealife, is the fact that the bark *Glenwood* sailed under sealed orders, her destination unknown until those orders were opened; or that the ship was struck twice by lightning on the voyage south, resulting in the death of one man. Nor did she relate that her youngest son Willie, the only one of her four children to accompany her on that cruise, fell mortally ill of yellow fever as they neared Pensacola Bay. All night long, as they lay hove to at Santa Rosa Island she was fighting for her son's life, while Confederate and Union gunboats dueled nearby. When the battle was over the *Glenwood* had survived unscathed, but little Willie was dead.

Mary Satterly Rowland must have agonized often that if she had not brought Willie along on the *Glenwood* his life might have been spared. Obviously, taking children to exotic ports involved the risk of exposing them to exotic diseases, too. For a mother who was a long distance away from the supporting domestic network of home, however, even the usual childhood ailments could prove alarming. Elizabeth, the second wife of Captain Benjamin Jones, who sailed with him on the *Tri-Mountain* for Chile and Peru, departing from New York on New Year's Day 1875, found herself nursing her children within two weeks of sailing. On Thursday January

7, "Bessie not well at night," wrote Mrs. Jones in her travel diary; "all broke out afraid she has scarlet fever." The diagnosis was wrong, for on the ninth she wrote, "Today quite pleasant Bessie had a very hot fever all night the flush has proved to be a rash and we have decided it is measles."

Measles, though a little less dangerous than scarlet fever, was even more contagious, so that all the children were laid low with fevers and rashes, succumbing one by one. "Florence has been sick all night with violent headache and pain in her back and side -- throat swollen,"

Marjorie Louise Wells, Caroline Adair Wells, and Robert Charles Wells with crewman on merchant schooner *Bertha L. Downs* out of Stony Brook, c. 1915
The children sailed with their parents, Captain Robert Francis Wells and Carrie Bantle Wells, until Marjorie had to go to school at age twelve. During years at sea, the children were taught by a tutor from Martinique - they all spoke French fluently. The children had pet goats, birds, and monkeys. One of their goats ate all the lace curtains that Carrie had made, another died when it fell into the engine room machinery. The crew made a canvas "aquarium" on deck for the children and filled it with tropical fish - one trip through the Sargasso Sea delighted the children when they netted thousands of baby fish and all manner of eels, crabs, etc.

Ellen Elizabeth Evans Jones, c.1915
Captain Benjamin Jones' first wife Mary died within a month of arriving back in New York, but loneliness drove him to take his second wife Elizabeth and their family to sea. Elizabeth survived, to become the mother and grandmother of a large family.

wrote Mrs. Jones on the 15th. "Carrie is vomiting," she went on, adding with a note of tired resignation, "and I presume she is coming down with measles." They all recovered, so that on January 23 their mother was able to write, "Children all on deck," but it is understandable that many seafaring wives chose to leave their young ones behind in the care of friends and relations, rather than run the risk of seeing the captain's quarters turn into a children's hospital, with no doctor on call and only one nurse (the mother herself) in attendance.

A merchant captain's wife whose seafaring career was greatly altered by her own bad health was Mary Swift Jones of the bark *Mary & Louisa*. When she embarked at New York she was already fatally ill with consumption, a disease that

Captain Rowland's spyglass
Model of the *Modesta*
Mary Satterly Rowland
Mary Satterly Rowland traveled on a number of vessels including her husband's last command, the *Modesta* (model shown above), becoming familiar with a host of exotic ports in Africa, the Mediterranean, and South America.

was to carry her off within a month of arriving back in New York in 1861. The voyage itself was unusual. The original plan had been a fast round-trip to Shanghai, returning with a cargo of tea. The masters of deep-sea merchants were just as vulnerable to shifts in markets as their coasting brothers, however, and so Mary's husband Captain Benjamin Jones signed a contract to sail short voyages between China and Japan. As time went by, Mary was forced to stop on shore with missionaries in Kanagawa, Japan, because of the progress of her disease.

She preferred to live on board when her husband was in port, but even when Benjamin was away Mary did not seem unhappy with her lot. In contrast to the whaling wives, who strongly resented being left on shore while their husbands went off to the northern Pacific a-whaling, merchant wives like Mary Jones and Mary Satterly Rowland enjoyed penning long descriptions of exotic surroundings for presumably admiring readers at home, taking patent pride in portraying themselves as seasoned travelers. "Had I wit enough I might write quite a book during my travels by sea and in Port, for I have some opportunity of seeing the different manners and customs of foreign Nations," mused Mary Satterly Rowland in a journal entry dated July 21, 1856, while traversing the Mediterranean.

"And I am sure – let me go where I may – I shall never see a more odd dress than is worn by the old Country frows [fraus] at Antwerp when they come into the City mornings to sell their Marketing, some of them riding about in small carts drawn by dogs... And then the wooden shoes and enormous white lace caps with such long broad ears to them, hanging down over their bosoms... and then their short petticoats, which are rather to short for the fashion of the Ladies of our Citys, who are not content unless their dress is draging on the ground behind them. These good old frows - O they did look so very laughable. A stranger can not keep a straight face and go amongst them, especially to the Market. The wooden shoes have to be very large in order not to pinch the foot, thus they slip on the heel at every step with a continual click clack from morning till Night. I should think it would be intolerable to wear them and have such a noise at their heels."

Similarly, on November 4, 1859, just after her first arrival in Yokohoma Harbor, Japan, Mary Swift Jones wrote in worldly-wise tones, "I have taken a great notice to go on shore lately... but were it not for the fine China handsome lacquered & cheap silks to be got I should hardly think it would pay to go on shore & be followed by 200 or 300 people on wooden shoes clattering after you they all acted afraid of me none would touch my clothes unless I gave them permission & while some examined my dress hat mantilla & gloves, one or two would commence fanning me they thought I must be almost roasted with so much clothes on."

In very similar vein, she wrote from Kanagawa to her sister Ellen in October 1860, "My carriage is a bamboo sedan chair, very much like a wheelbarrow with the wheel off & shafts behind as well as front, this I fill with cushions, send for coolies & as I am a foreigner I must have three, one a government man, to receive the money, steady the chair, pick flowers or grass, & try to make me

talk Japanese... I think the country the most beautiful I ever saw," she went on:

It may be because [it is] so different. Sicily gives an idea of grandeur, one feels as though nature herself looked forth in gloomy grandeur from her rent rocks & valleys while every snowy mountain top & fertile lowland of Mediterranean Europe tells of ages & of races that have passed, and in magnificent tropical Brazil I fancy nature looks as she did before the hand of the white man laid hold of it, but in looking at the hills of Nagasaki (not walking up them) & riding out behind Kanagawa, its quiet sunny beauty has impressed me with a feeling of rest & quiet that I fancy I shall feel nowhere else but at home."

Similarly, Mary Satterly Rowland, musing over the many ports and places she had seen in a sea letter begun for her sister Hannah in January 1873, wrote, "I hardly know what place to call my home, it seems to be my lot to spend much of my time on the sea and in many Climes and yet I am allways at home in fact I am quite a cosmopolite." Then, later in the same long letter, she elaborated on the theme, saying, "I manage to go around onshore more or less in every Port and learn the different manners and customs of different Nations and the works of God & Man both Nature and Art and find much to amuse edify and interest us and see what so many Travelers pay large sums for while H[enry] makes us a living and the Brig is our Hotell and even what is much better our Home while we travel."

Typically, however, both women followed up such remarks with the hasty assurance that they had traveled only to be with their husbands, and of course

Picture of a Sunday in Yokohama (detail) c.1860
Artist: Sadahide

Sails Returning to the Landing Pier (View of an American couple in Yokohama) c.1860
Artist: : Yoshitora
Mary Swift Jones was among the first westerners to live in the treaty ports of Japan. Japanese artists depicted the clothing and customs of Europeans and Americans in highly popular wood block prints.

were always homesick. It was as if they were afraid that the longed-for letters would stop arriving if the folks got the impression that they were too worldly-wise to require any news of home. "You must not fail to write me a long letter as soon as you receive this," wrote Mary Swift Jones to her sister Ellen; "I like to get letters from you all," wrote Mary Satterly Rowland to her daughters from the port of London, June 17, 1866.

The seafaring wives – not excluding Carrie Davis, who never sailed further than a few hours from home – wrote assiduously themselves, and felt justified in expecting letters in return. However, there were problems. Quite apart from the long time the blue-water sailors had to wait for news (Mary Swift Jones pointed out to her sister Eliza that "it takes a letter from 65 to 75 days to reach us from N.Y."), in faraway lands they found that sending mail was not as easy as it was back in Long Island, for the recipients often had to pay the postage. "I have taken advantage of your letter," wrote Mary Swift Jones to her sister, "to send one to Eliza and a note to Amelia if the postage is double make them pay half, if I could I would prepay the postage, but it would seldom make any difference but I will set that straight when I come home." Mail, alternatively, was entrusted to cooperative captains who were bound for New York, but such fellows were often not easily found.

Thoughts of home were more heartfelt still if children had been left behind, and when the voyage was an extended one the temptation to take the whole family was great. Quite apart from the dangers of seafaring, it was a difficult decision to make, however, for children who grew up in such an unnatural environment tended to become unmanageable, particularly the boys, who could flee into the rigging to escape lessons or an irate mother. The whaling wife Mary Lawrence remarked in Honolulu on November 4, 1857, that Captain and Mrs. Homer of the merchant ship *Messenger-Bird* had two children with them, "one little boy four years of age who swears

View of Yokohama Harbor
Map of Japan from Captain Benjamin Jones' atlas
Mary Swift Jones, first wife of Captain Benjamin Jones, was forced by declining health to live on shore in Japan, where she resided at the mission house at Kanagawa, now in the district of Yokohama.

equal to any man that I ever heard in my life. He made nothing of repeating an oath to his mother," expostulated Mrs. Lawrence in open horror. "How she could bear it I cannot tell, but it made the tears start to my eyes." Mary Lurch Bayles, who had been voyaging with her husband Captain Edward Post Bayles on the *Lavinia Belle* for fourteen years, gave up sailing when her son Hagen tried to push his younger brother Edward out of a port hole in shark-infested Havana Harbor.

The alternative was to leave the children at home in the care of relatives, and this sometimes proved to be a fortunate choice. Clarissa King Wicks of Seaford in Nassau County left her baby George with her in-laws when she took passage to join her husband in the Pacific, and thus saved the child's life, for the packet foundered off Cape Horn with the loss of all on board. Nevertheless, it was a very hard decision to make, for men as well as women. A particularly poignant story is told of Captain "Big Manuel" Enos of Cold Spring Harbor, who sailed in command of the whaleship *Java* on a four-year voyage in 1864, leaving his four-year-old daughter Melna behind with his wife Susan, who was pregnant. While he was away Melna died, and when he returned the baby, Ella Nora, was four years old. Captain Enos did not realize the difference until he was told, and was understandably grieved and confused.

The death of a child left at home for the child's own protection was a particularly cruel irony, and a constant dread of the seafaring wives, so much so that Carrie Hubbard Davis gave up sailing when she bore a much adored son in 1884, even though her trips were by no means wide-ranging. This retirement from the sea was probably rather to her mother's chagrin, for Jane Culver Hubbard used her correspondence with her daughter to keep abreast of her husband's maritime concerns. On October 9, 1878, for instance, Carrie wrote to her mother in Southampton, reporting, "We went from Norwich to New London last Fri-

day – Saturday arrived at Orient about noon. We had favorable winds so the trip was not lengthy. Monday, we went up to New Suffolk, if we had not, I expected to write to you that day.

"Yesterday, they took over two hundred bushels of potatoes aboard – In the morning we came down to Orient – They expect to take some onions aboard here if they can get them, and some cabbage –

"I don't know whether we shall get away before Saturday or not - the weather is lowery now," she added – and so her mother was kept fully aware of what was going on, and could take part in family decisions.

Similarly, through her letters to her daughters Mary Emma, aged thirteen at the time, and Henrietta, aged eleven, Mary Satterly Rowland attempted to run the family farm in Setauket from afar. "I hope the Goslings will live and that Watson [the farmhand] will raise a good many chickens with you all to help," she penned in London on June 17, 1866.

I expect Mrs Hopkins [the housekeeper] makes a good deal of butter now will make considerable to sell sometime later when all the cows have calves... Pa says tell Watson he wants him to keep 8 pigs and Grand Pa can do what he thinks best with the others keep the best ones ourselves to keep over so we will not have to buy Pork next year and lard... I would like very much to have some of our good cherries hope there will be a good many Watson will pick them and Granma said she would come over and help Mrs Hopkins if she wanted her to fill up the empty jars dont let them be forget and those pears are very nice if she will please to preserve some...

"You can read this to Mrs. H[opkins]," Mrs. Rowland added, probably unnecessarily, for it is obvious for whom the stream of instructions was really intended. Perhaps, however, when the girls received a directive penned in a later letter, which ran, "dont let a lot of kittens live to make trouble drown them at once then you wont mind it," they neglected to pass it on to Mrs. Hopkins!

Captain Benjamin Jones and Mary Swift Jones

FORTY LITTLE RHYMES

D. Lothrop & Co.
Boston Mass

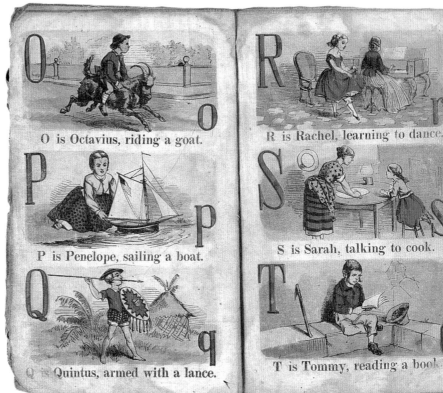

O is Octavius, riding a goat.

P is Penelope, sailing a boat.

Q is Quintus, armed with a lance.

R is Rachel, learning to dance.

S is Sarah, talking to cook.

T is Tommy, reading a book.

CHIT CHAT STORIES

FOR LITTLE FOLKS

Children's toys and Woodhull Rowland
What with cramped quarters, a rolling ship, and sailors trying to sleep at most times of the day, entertaining a young family was no easy task for the seafaring wife and mother.

Many of the sister sailors, however, had little choice about bringing up children on shipboard, for giving birth on a long voyage was just another hazard. "the Capt Wif gave birth to a child... Latitude 25.50 North, Long by D Re 75.45W" runs the entry for October 21, 1857, in the logbook of the brig *Thomas W. Rowland* to mark the birth of Mary Satterly Rowland and Captain Henry's son Woodhull Satterly. This presented an immediate problem, babies being apt to cry, and the four-hour rotation of watches on deck and watches below meaning that at any given time about half the crew was off-duty and trying to sleep. "I have to devise all sorts of plans of amusement to keep peace and quietness when the mates are below," wrote Mary Rowland, "and who ever heard of keeping children quiet." In port, too, small children precluded the social round of visiting, shopping, and sightseeing that child-free women enjoyed. Children born on voyage were invariably welcome, however, for the work and fun they entailed enlivened the seafaring life of the mother considerably. It was the reason many young mothers like Mary Satterly Rowland took their children to sea when small, leaving them behind only when schooling – and farm affairs – rendered it advisable.

With such pressing matters to be attended to at home, along with the risks ever present at sea, it does seem strange that the merchant husbands should invite their wives on voyage. Their situation was different from their whaling brothers, for merchant voyages seldom involved the four or five years that a Pacific whaling cruise entailed. Unlike bay coasterwomen such as Carrie Hubbard Davis, the merchant wives had little to do, apart from playing the part of hostess if any passengers were carried, and providing companionship for the captain, for there was a sea cook to do the cooking, and a steward to look after the cabins. Even if the women were accustomed to servants (for many of the merchant wives came from affluent families) there was nothing resembling the round of social visits and good works that made them feel of use at home. In a word, except for the tense times of storms and crew troubles and childbirth and illness, life at sea was boring.

Fred Essex, the man who took passage

on the *Emma T. Crowell* in Shanghai, penned an account that aptly illustrates how difficult it could be to pass the monotonous hours of fair weather passage. "I found it very hard to amuse myself from day-to-day..." he admitted.

The captain was a wonderful and enthusiastic hand at knitting slippers. I would sit and chaff with him till he got his pattern all wrong and had to unpick very likely half a day's work, and then I would go and see who else I could worry. Miss Pendleton [the captain's 18-year-old daughter Marietta] would be perhaps on deck near the wheel trying to teach her young brother his lessons. I would get up a little pantomime chasing the cat out on the stays; direct the boy's attention and bust the lesson.

"I had a wonderful influence on young Andrew," Essex modestly confessed. "I could excite him till he would whoop and holloa and fly round, wake up the watch below and scare his father, mother and sister up on deck to see he was not jumping overboard."

At no time, however, did Fred describe what Mrs. Pendleton did to pass the lagging time. No doubt, like Mary Rowland on board the brig *Thomas W. Rowland*, she sewed a great deal, and perhaps like Mary, too, she kept a journal. "I have got my Children asleep and now have sat down to write a little for my own satisfaction," Mary Rowland noted on December 9, 1855, "which is of no importance but answers to pass away Idle moments better than to sit with folded hands." Without her children to keep her occupied, she was very idle indeed.

"Those whose sea travelling experiences only extend to steamers can hardly grasp the exigencies of providing the necessities of life on a sailing vessel," Fred Essex opined, and many sister sailors would have heartily agreed with him, removed from the supporting domestic circle of home as they were, waiting out the days of passage until they could enjoy the exotic sights and shopping in some far-off foreign port.

And yet they sailed, and kept on sailing as long as the circling winds carried merchantmen around the world. Even after

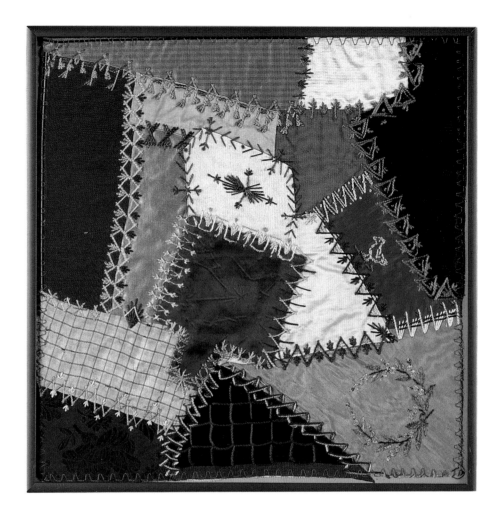

Mary Swift Jones's early death Captain Benjamin Jones felt a constant need for a wife at sea. "Somethink [*sic*] reminds of her every day In Shanghai and when in Japan," he wrote to his sister on June 3, 1868. "I feel her loss more at sea than at any other time... when alone I get to thinking of her I go away back to the first time I saw her in [the] schoolroom. I think you remember the time as I was very ackcious to know who she was." Then he wrote to his brother-in-law "Scud" Jayne, declaring, "I must find a companion suitable for going to sea."

Little wonder, then, that he was remarried not long after arriving home, to the daughter of the Setauket Presbyterian Church minister, Elizabeth Evans; or that he carried her to sea; or that the couple took at least three of their four children along, just like hundreds of Elizabeth's sister sailors.

Benjamin's reason was very plain. It was the same motive that drove them all: the pure and simple loneliness of a bluewater seaman at sea.

Without children, however, time hung heavy for the captain's wife at sea. Many hours were filled with sewing and other handiwork - such as the crazy quilt block pictured at the top of the page, part of the work accomplished by Elizabeth Evans Jones, pictured above.

The *Petticoat Whalers of Long Island*

by Joan Druett

Ships Gamming
Artist: : Ron Druett
Gamming, where two ships hauled aback and hove to and parties rowed from one vessel to the other to pay mid-sea visitors, was a social custom peculiar to the whalemen.

On November 21, 1850, in the middle of the Pacific Ocean, the young steerage boy of the whaleship *Hannibal* of New London, Connecticut, noted in his journal that they had spoken to the *Huntsville* of Cold Spring Harbor, New York. Such an event was certainly worth recording. For whalemen who had been many months from home, to hear the lookout at the masthead call out that he had raised a sail was a very welcome interruption in the tedious routine of looking for whales. Steerage boy Nat Morgan, earlier in his journal, described the dialogue that followed:

"Where away?" cries the captain.
"Three points off the lee bow, sir."
"And what does she look like?"

If the answer to this was, "A whaler, sir," the excitement became intense. Signals were exchanged in a flurry of flags, and the downwind ship would lay her fore yard aback, coming to a near standstill with her sails pulling against each other. Then the windward ship swept down to her, bowsprit aimed at the stilled ship's waist, a dramatic process that required nerves of steel and a firm hand on the helm. At the ultimate second, just as collision seemed unavoidable, the moving ship would brace up so that she sheered past the other's stern, so close that the two captains, standing on the quarterdeck or on top of the "hurricane house" that sheltered the helm, could converse in almost normal tones.

"Ship ahoy," says the stranger.
"Hello."
"What ship is that?"
"The *Hannibal* of New London."

This was the start of a ritualistic exchange, with the same questions being asked even if the captains were brothers, or had seen each other the day before. First, they would exchange reports, and so the crew of the *Hannibal* found out that Captain Freeman H. Smith had enjoyed a most successful voyage, for he reported 3,400 barrels of whale oil taken, though just 13 months away from home.

If the *Hannibal* had had a poor report, this enviable news probably would have finished the conversation and ended the encounter. However, Captain Sluman Gray had been equally lucky in the Arctic, and so he lingered, to inform Captain Smith that Sarah Gray was on board. "By jolly," Captain Freeman H. Smith of the *Huntsville* perhaps exclaimed, "that's a fine coincidence, for I carry my wife as well." And at once, on behalf of himself and his wife Cordelia, he issued an invitation to Captain and Sarah Gray to come on board of his ship for a "gam."

Gamming, which involved a timespan of hours or even days, as the whaleboats were lowered and pulled from ship to ship so that everyone either visited or received visitors, was a custom peculiar to the whalemen. While merchant ships did speak, it was done hurriedly, for they had tight schedules to keep, and were intent on reaching port with the minimum of interruption. And so they seldom stopped to socialize, even if the captain was one of the many who carried his wife on voyage. The whalemen, by contrast, were cruising back and forth in their endless hunt for their quarry, going into port as infrequently as possible, not turning for home until their holds were full of oil, a goal which could take several years to attain. Of all the seamen, they were the loneliest by far, and so, hungry for company and conversation, they visited each other often and at length, so that not infrequently clusters of several ships all a-gamming together were recorded.

Gams were more than enjoyable get-togethers, however. They were a good opportunity for catching up on whaling gossip, when news of other whaleships and whaling grounds was exchanged. And, even more importantly, if the other ship hailed from the same port or even the same state, it was the time to catch up, too, on longed-for news of home. To understand this fully, it must be realized that whaling at its most successful was a village industry, involving the whole of the home community. The reason New England dominated American whaling was because the townsfolk were prepared to devote the necessary concentration of resources into the perilous and unpredictable business. They provided the ships, the money, the ponderous, specialized, and very expensive whaling gear, and in the early years they provided nearly all of the crews. On the 1839 voyage of the Sag Harbor ship *Thomas Dickason*, for example, the crewlist was composed almost entirely of men from the Hamptons, with names like Babcock, Miller, Edwards, and Havens (Wickham Havens was the master), a comradely lot who held singalongs in the cabin and made candy in the galley as they cruised the wide Pacific for whales. Captain Samuel Pierson recruited more than half his crews in his home village of Bridgehampton, and when the *Salem* sailed out of Sag Harbor in 1844 with

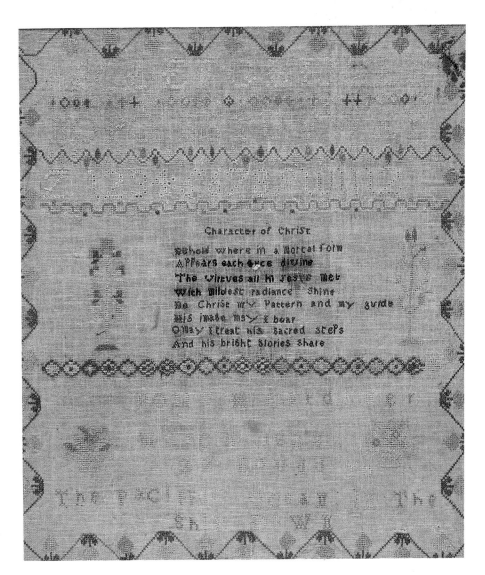

Captain David Hand in command, nineteen of the twenty-eight men on board hailed from Long Island, two of them Shinnecock Indians.

Little wonder, then, that the whalemen actively sought out whaleships from their own region for companionship. New Bedforders stuck together and likewise Nantucket men, gamming, sailing, and whaling in groups. The Connecticut masters are another example. According to the account kept on the California ground from October 1846 to March 1847 by Mary, wife of Captain William Brewster, the seven ships the *Tiger* gammed with were all from her home state of Connecticut, two from the Brewsters' home village of Stonington.

Polly Gardiner, wife of Captain "Harry" Gardiner, accompanied her husband on a Pacific voyage on the whaleship *Dawn*, departing from the port of New York on Christmas Day, 1826. She left an enduring memento of this remarkable excursion, completing a sampler with the alphabet and numerals and a religious verse, by filling in the spare space on the bottom with her name, the date - "March 16, 1828" amended to "1827," and the cross-stitched words, "Bound to the Pacific Ocean in the ship Dawn."

Captain Henry Gardiner of Quogue Wedding ring for Polly (Mrs. Henry) Gardiner

Captain Henry Gardiner's logbook on the 1821-24 voyage of the whaleship *Dawn* of New York has his wife Polly's name written in the margins so often that it is not surprising that he took her along on the next voyage of the same ship, leaving New York on Christmas Day 1826. Polly left a most unusual record of her seafaring, a sampler on which she embroidered the words "Bound to the Pacific Ocean in the ship Dawn."

Gamming Chair

Whaling lore has it that a Captain's wife would be lowered to the boat for a gam in a half-barrel chair known as a "gamming chair." In practice these were unwieldy, often dumping the occupant, so it is most likely that the ladies stepped into the boat from deck and were lowered in the boat.

By this means the whalemen were able to recreate, if only for a little while, an acceptable facsimile of the hamlet back home – and Long Island men were no exception. On February 25, 1860, for instance, the log-keeper of the Sag Harbor whaleship *Mary Gardiner* recorded speaking with the ships *Excel* and *Noble*, also of that port: "a general gam," he wrote; "the Capts on board of the M. Gardiner the mates on board of the Excel the Second mates on board of the Noble. Merry times these." Similarly, when the *Salem* of Sag Harbor arrived at the Hawaiian Islands in January 1846, Captain David Hand and his crew were delighted to rendezvous with the *Thomas Dickason*, the *Huron*, the *Acasta*, and the *Levant*, all of Sag Harbor, the brig *Washington* of Greenport, and the *Richmond* and the *Splendid*, both of Cold Spring Harbor.

And the brave women who accompanied their husbands on the long whaling voyages felt exactly the same way about gamming, both at sea and in port. The pleasure of gamming was a major topic in the journals they wrote, and in the letters they sent back home, and the gam

was even better if the folks on the other ship came from somewhere near the place that they called "home." Caroline Rose of Southampton, who sailed on three voyages over nearly two decades (1853 to 1871), remembered her gams with such clarity that in old age she borrowed the official log of her last excursion, the 1865 voyage of the *Trident*, and she and her daughter Emma consulted and reminisced as Emma copied it out, adding personal notations. At the end of the entry for June 27, 1866, for instance, Emma noted that "Capt. Raynor of the Raindeer [*sic*] had his wife and two Children, George & Grace" on board. This was definitely memorable, for not only had it meant that Emma (nine years old at the time) had had other young people to play with, but it had provided a most welcome chance to hear news of home, for though they sailed on a New Bedford ship (as, indeed, the Roses did), Captain George Raynor and his young wife Adelaide hailed from Long Island.

However, while talking with folks from home was an unforgettable treat, any gam at all was welcome to the women, just as it was with the men. When the ship *Dawn* of New York put into San Salvador for repairs in 1827, Polly Hubbard Gardiner, the wife of Captain Harry Gardiner of Quogue, Long Island, was delighted to find a brig just in from the Indian Ocean in port. "The capt's wife was with him," wrote the ship's carpenter, Will Latimer, "and as our capt. also had his wife there was considerable 'gamming' as sailors call it."

The women's gamming was certainly not restricted to visiting each other in port. Despite hoops and hampering skirts the enterprising ladies clambered in and out of boats to pay eager visits on other women, and it made no difference if they were perfect strangers to each other. Not only did the sister sailors have much in common, but each was psychologically prepared to *like* the other woman immensely. "Capt. Gray and his wife went aboard and stayed till 10 in the evening," wrote steerage boy Nathaniel Morgan on the *Hannibal*. "Capt. Smith has his wife, and Doctor King and wife on board as passengers - Expect we shall have to keep company for a week or so in order to let the women *gam* - for they beat all for visiting and especially at sea."

According to whaling legend, the captain's wife was lowered in and out of the boats in a "gamming chair," which swung from ropes secured to the main yard. This, however, was not quite the truth. Chairs were made, and tried out, but proved to be both terrifying and risky. Not only did they giddily spin, but control of the ropes was precarious. According to the reminiscences of Jamie Earle, who spent part of his childhood on the *Charles W. Morgan*, the occupant was liable to be "dunked" in the sea. And so, it is much more likely that Sarah Gray stepped over the rail into the slung starboard quarter boat, and was lowered that way, just as Cordelia Smith probably was, when she and her husband repaid the visit by going on board the *Hannibal* next day.

As it happens, young Nat Morgan was rather unkind about the lengthy gam that the women enjoyed. "At 4 AM the steward and boy were set to scouring the cabin and the crew scrubbing decks with lie [lye] and cinders – All hands grumbling and cursing the Huntsville for this job," he groused. "At 8 AM ran down to the H. and found Capt. S. and wife and Mr. King and wife already to come aboard – they came aboard and stayed all day – and such a time – more affectation and soft soap than would fill a slush tub. Nobody seemed to live on this globe but they and no dinner for us until 2 o'clock. They left at 7 PM amid such a scene and soft soap and kissing it made us all sick – Agreed to keep company and have another *gam* tomorrow – go ahead." Not only was the *Hannibal* homeward bound and every man anxious to get there, but the *Huntsville* was not a Connecticut ship.

Cordelia Smith's situation, however, was an illustration of a problem that faced most of the Long Island whaling wives. Like all her sister whalers, Cordelia certainly deserved her gams. She must have felt her heart quail when she first took up residence on her husband's ship, for while whalers were fairly substantial vessels (the *Huntsville* was rated at 523 tons compared to the *Hannibal*'s 441, which was closer to the average), a large crew of about 30 men lived aboard, every one of whom needed some space to sleep. The between-decks space was also limited by the large amidships "blubber room," which was reserved for cutting up tons of fat from slaughtered whales.

Not only were the after cabins cramped, but they were not at all luxurious, lacking anything more than the most superficial decoration. Unless she had her own small room on deck, the only private

Whaleship messroom of the *Charles W. Morgan*
The foreward cabin of a whaler had to be shared with three or four mates or officers and on some whalers with the boatsteerers as well.

area the whaling wife possessed was the narrow stateroom she shared with her husband, along with a tiny (six feet by eight feet) sitting room, set across the stern, which was crammed with a heavy sofa and chart table and chair. Meals were eaten in the "forward cabin," which was almost filled with a massive table that had to be shared with the three or four mates, who were often not very cultivated fellows. Polly Gardiner did not just have to put up with a hard-drinking crew, but the food on the table ran out as well, with the result that in the South China Sea so many of the crew were laid low with the deficiency disease scurvy, that until they raised a small island and took life-saving fruit and vege-

tables on board, there were not able-bodied men enough to tack the ship.

If that were not sufficiently daunting, there was always the depressing reminder that Pacific whalers were not supposed to steer for home until each and every barrel in the capacious hold was full. Both Sarah Gray and Cordelia Smith had much reason to congratulate themselves that their husbands had been so fortunate in the whale hunt, for filling the ship within eighteen months of leaving home was very rare indeed by the 1840s. Carolyn Lowen, who sailed from Sag Harbor with her second husband, Captain James Madison Tabor, for a "honeymoon cruise" on the whaleship

Eliza Wheeler Edwards

Eliza Edwards was 27 years old when, on August 20, 1857, she took passage from New York to Honolulu, to meet up with her husband Eli, who was master of the *Black Eagle* of Sag Harbor. Over the next two years she became close friends with many of her "sister sailors" in the Hawaiian Islands, traveling from island to island on local schooners, and sampling life in Honolulu, Lahaina, and Hilo. Because her husband was unlucky with his ships, Eliza did not return home to Sag Harbor until 1860, when Eli was the first mate of the *Splendid* of Cold Spring Harbor. Captain Samuel Pierson, commander of the *Splendid*, was so pleased to have her on board that he gave her the captain's accommodations, refurbished for her comfort.

Augusta, on July 24, 1857, did not arrive home until January 19, 1861, and Roxanna Green, who sailed on the *Sheffield* of Cold Spring Harbor in 1854, was away for fifty-six months – long enough to have a baby on board, despite being fifty-two years old.

And, despite the many romantic tales, a whaleship was no place for. a lady. Not only were the quarters cramped, the company rough, and the trade both gruesome and dangerous, but because the ships sailed slowly in search of whales, they rolled a great deal, with much washing back and forth of the bilges, and so most whaling wives were terribly seasick, often for months on end. Worst of all, perhaps, were the lagging years of loneliness. While Dr. King (originally of Nantucket, but now an entrepreneur in California) and his wife were on board the *Huntsville* at the time of the gam with the *Hannibal*, it was very unusual for whalers to carry passengers any distance. The captains would have enjoyed the extra money as much as their wives would have appreciated the society, no doubt, but it was practical only when on passage, for the rest of the time the ships were beating back and forth on the same patch of ocean, endlessly quartering the sea in the search for whales. Gray did ferry a few from New London to the Azores at the start of this particular voyage, and when they left the ship on October 2, 1849, Nat Morgan recorded that "The lady passengers were much affected on leaving Mrs. Gray, and she and they shed tears rather profusely."

Obviously, there were great differences between the whaling vessels and the blue-water merchant ships, for the latter boasted not just fine, spacious accommodations, but traveled swiftly from port to port, and often carried passengers. On board a merchantman the captain's wife might be idle and bored, but at least she could dress up and play the part of gracious hostess. The whaling master's wife, by contrast, lived a strange solitary kind of existence, surrounded by men and yet alone, forced to find some way of passing away the dragging years

while she waited for the ship to fill up with oil.

So why did whaling masters like Freeman Smith and Sluman Gray decide to take their wives on a voyage? Coming from Connecticut made a difference, for the earliest whaling wives were almost all from that state, eight of them from the one port of New London. Sarah Frisbee Gray was one of those original seafarers, voyaging first on the *Newburyport* of Stonington in 1844. In October 1846, she encountered another Stonington wife, Mary Brewster of the *Tiger*. "She was a sister sailor," wrote Mrs. Brewster in her journal after the meeting – a catchy phrase, used often from then on, for Mrs. Brewster, Sarah Gray, and their sister sailors of the 1840s were the women who set off the wife-carrying fashion, which reached full flight in the 1850s and persevered for the next thirty years.

By logic, therefore, Connecticut women like Sarah Gray and Mrs. Brewster had a very good chance of gamming with women from their own home state. Unfortunately for the whaling wives of New York, however, the growth of the wife-carrying fad coincided with the lapse of Long Island whaling. Up until 1845 Sag Harbor had been one of the five major whaling ports of the world, but in that year a disastrous fire swept the waterfront, and by the time rebuilding was finished the young men of the town were off about another adventure, responding to the call of gold in California. And so, the industry in Sag Harbor never became fully re-established.

This meant that relatively few Long Island women went a-whaling, though those from Sag Harbor were supplemented by a handful of similarly brave souls from Greenport and Cold Spring Harbor. In direct contrast, Nantucket whaling wives arrived in such numbers on the whaling grounds off Chile and Peru in the 1850s that they were able to recreate many aspects of the domestic circle back home, calling on each other, sharing "receipts" and crochet patterns, nursing each other when ill, delivering babies, making quilts, knitting for infants. Many lived next-door to each other back in "Scrap Island," and many were related by birth or marriage. A duplication of the domestic circle back home was virtually impossible for the Long Island whaling wives, however, simply because of lack of numbers. In 1857, when Mrs. William James Grant of the *Huntsville* of Cold Spring Harbor and Mrs. Eliza Edwards of the *Black Eagle* of Sag Harbor waited in Honolulu for their husbands to return from the northern whaling season, they were very lucky to have each other for company, and, what's more, to be able to board at the house kept by Mrs. Cartwright, the wife of one of the settlers, who was a Shelter Island man. Other Long Island wives were not nearly as fortunate, and so there was a tendency to seek out the companionship of ladies from Connecticut. Not only did the Connecticut women have much more experience of seafaring, but back home they were almost neighbors. Thus, Elizabeth Chapman Green of Southampton, who sailed with her husband James on the *Nimrod* in 1851, boarded in Lahaina, Maui, with Mrs. Thomas Long of New London; and in September 1847 Elizabeth's sister-in-law Maria, wife of Captain Barney Green of the Sag Harbor whaleship *Ontario*, "cruised" the stores of Honolulu in company with Mary Brewster of Stonington.

Another Long Islander left on shore in Hawaii was Emmeline Winters of Sag Harbor. On July 23, 1848, at the age of 29, she sailed with her husband Captain Jonas Winters on the *Elizabeth Frith*. The expedition was a typically village-oriented venture, for two of Emmeline's brothers-in-law, Charles and Silas Winters, were numbered in the crew of mostly Hampton men, and so the departure from Long Wharf was an emotional occasion. According to an account in the Sag Harbor *Express*, the pilot boat that accompanied the ship out of the harbor was crowded with a large party of friends, who sang songs of farewell and offered prayers for the success of the

Hawaiian Scenes
Because whaleships called often at Honolulu, Hilo, and Lahaina, the whaling wives became familiar with the tropical way of life, living in airy houses, sleeping under mosquito nets, feasting on native food and exploring active volcanoes.

voyage, while a Bible was presented to the captain's wife.

Despite this bright and hopeful start, the voyage did not go well. When the *Elizabeth Frith* arrived at Honolulu on February 20, 1849, Emmeline Winters was put on shore there, to wait as comfortably as she could for the birth of a son, Clarence Madison, her second child. Meanwhile, Captain Jonas Winters proceeded to the icy Arctic Ocean, meeting up with another brother, Philander, who was in command of the *Richmond* of Cold Spring Harbor.

In August, the *Richmond* went ashore in a dense fog, and was lost. The officers and crew escaped to land, and were kindly treated by the natives. Eventually they were rescued by Captain Tinker of the *Junior* of New Bedford, Captain Hallock (one of Emmeline's relatives) of the *Panama* of Sag Harbor, and Jonas Winters of the *Elizabeth Frith*. Philander was taken on board of his brother's ship, and died of grief and apoplexy on the passage from the Straits to the Sandwich Islands. Emmeline did not hear of the calamity until October, when the *Eliza-*

beth Frith arrived back in port.

Another to find herself stranded "in circumstances" was an Orienter, Martha Brown, who sailed with her husband Captain Edwin Peter Brown on the *Lucy Ann* of Greenport, leaving home on August 21, 1847. She was twenty-six years old, and had left a two-year-old daughter, Ella, behind. Just four days after departure she had her first chance to gam, for a second vessel from Greenport, the *Roanoke*, joined them. The two ships sailed in company to Fayal, in the Azores, and then went their separate ways.

The master of the *Roanoke* was Captain Smith Baldwin of Shelter Island, who carried his twenty-three-year-old bride of three months, Maria Cartwright Baldwin. Maria was a resourceful young woman, who eventually learned to handle the vessel so well that she would take the helm when tacking ship. Her first child was born at St. Helena, where they stopped for ten days, delaying the ship just long enough to christen the baby "Ella," perhaps because Martha had spoken of her own little Ella so often, or

Martha Smith Brewer Brown
On August 31, 1847, Martha Brown sailed from Orient on the ship *Lucy Ann* to go a-whaling with her husband, leaving her young daughter Ella with relatives. Lonely and un-happy on board ship, she did her best to make the best of her strange adventure, until her husband Edwin left her on shore in Honolulu, to cope as well as she could with pregnancy and a greater loneliness than ever before.

perhaps after Eleanor Carroll, the American consul's wife in that place. Martha, by contrast, was confined in Honolulu, Hawaii, after being deposited there, alone and friendless, a full five months before her term.

Up until March 1848, Martha had managed to be reasonably content on voyage, bolstered by her faith in God and her open affection for her husband. "If quince groves and moon light nights are incentives to make love, surely moon light nights on ship bord [*sic*] are doubly so," she wrote on October 18, 1847. Alas, the moonlit nights had their natural effect. In April 1848 Martha found herself on shore in Honolulu, left amongst strangers to cope with an inconvenient pregnancy. Understandably, she felt angry, and very frightened about how she would cope. "This is not my

home and I do not know of one here that I can call my friend," she accused Edwin, in the first shore entry (April 30) of a diary-letter she kept for him to read when he returned.

Captain Edwin Brown did have his reasons for abandoning her. Whaleships, traditionally, did not carry surgeons, the master being the fellow in charge of the medical chest, so no doubt he felt a little queasy at the thought of delivering a baby on board ship. Martha did not share his qualms, and so the rest of her journal makes remarkable reading, for Martha Brown was an unusual woman who wrote openly and earthily, with none of the mincing inhibitions that are more usually associated with women of her era. "You would take very little pride in my form at present, unless it was because people would be led to judge that you was 'miki' [miti: good, virile], as the natives say," she penned on June 25. Likewise, she made no bones about letting Edwin know exactly how she felt.

Because he had left her without enough money, Martha was forced to board some distance out of town. This was yet another source of resentment, for she noted on July 5 that, "I regret very much that I am up in the valley ... [because] I cannot see my Sisters but seldom, for so we call ourselves." These sisters, "or Brother whaleman's wives, rather" included Jane Gelett and Mrs. Young of the New Bedford vessels *Uncas* and *Abigail*, and Sarah Gray of the *Jefferson* of New London - the same Sarah Gray who sailed on the *Hannibal* next voyage, to share that long gam with Cordelia Smith of the Cold Spring Harbor vessel *Huntsville* in November 1850.

In view of the Long Island wives' affinity with women from Connecticut, it is no great surprise that Martha Brown and Sarah Gray immediately struck up a friendship, despite their very different situations. "Capt. Gray told his wife when he left her to try to take comfort and enjoy herself," Martha bitterly penned on July 20; "and as far as money and credit would go, not to scrimp herself. She is not in circumstances. My Husband left me in one of the most unpleasent situation a Lady can be left in, without her husband, and among strangers, with the request that I would do my washing myself – a thing which no other American Lady does, not even the mision Ladies....

"You also requested that I would not buy anything but what I positively needed," she pursued on an even more personal and accusing note; "I think I have done so... [and] feel evry day almost that I recieve slights because I cannot dress in silks and nice cloth[e]s. Before Mrs. Gray came I felt alone. Now I feel that in her I have a true friend, although she far exceeds me in dress and show... I do not know how it is with you, but I know I wish I was with you on board the *Lucy Ann*. There I should not have to spend anything," she pointed out with sharp logic.

Such plainly expressed rebellion, while it confirms the impression of Martha Brown's open, down-to-earth character, jibes very oddly with our modern concept of the ideal woman of Martha's time. That Captain Brown himself held strong opinions on the place and proper nature of women is evidenced by a note he pencilled into the logbook he kept that voyage, apparently during an introspective moment. "There are many qualifications in A woman's character which renders them objects of love & admiration," he mused. "I need not specify for we all know them," he went on, but nevertheless itemized a few, including, "A meek & quiet disposition." Back in Honolulu, however, Martha was feeling neither meek nor quiet. "Must I be confined without my husband or one that I can call my friend," she demanded on August 20, just a week before her term.

A friend did come to her aid, however, her "sister" from Connecticut, Sarah Gray, the nearest approach that Martha had to the supporting domestic circle of home. "Mrs. Grey was with me dureing my confinement and did for me and my

Captain Jetur Rose and his wife Caroline
Artist: Ron Druett
Lauded as the Belle of Southampton in her youth, Caroline Rose nevertheless sailed with her husband for 14 years, giving birth in Honolulu and raising her daughter Emma on shipboard, despite the disapproval of the missionaries.

child, as an own sister would have done," Martha recorded a month after the event. Naturally, both women "felt very bad," when the *Jefferson* sailed from Honolulu for home, Captain Sluman Gray having returned from the northern whaling ground in October. "When we left the ship," Martha related October 16, "she stood waving her pockethanderchief [*sic*] and crying. She is a nice woman – has one of the kindest hearts a human being ever possesed. The least I can say of her is I love her like a Sister."

Captain Edwin Peter Brown was apparently in no hurry to get back to Honolulu, for he did not arrive to collect his wife and infant son until November 11, nearly a full month after the Grays had sailed. He arrived so much later than the rest of the whaling fleet, in fact, that Martha held grave fears for his safety. Indeed, his behavior throughout begs the question: why did he ever conclude to take his wife Martha on voyage?

It surely was a grave decision to make, one that should have demanded much forethought. Obviously, the hazards for a woman of going a-whaling included much more than being set ashore to get on with an inconvenient pregnancy. Not only was whaling itself very dangerous, but a whaling sister had to face the "normal" hazards of a life at sea as well. Sarah Eliza Jennings of Sag Harbor was on board the *Mary Gardiner* of Sag Harbor in 1861 when the ship was chased for more than two hours by a Confederate raider, and Elizabeth White of Cold Spring Harbor was on board the *Courser* off the coast of Chile in 1873, when the whaler was rammed and sunk by the steamship *Ytata*.

Renowned as the "Belle of Southampton" before her marriage to Captain Jetur Rose, Caroline Rose had been feted for her perfect, cultured manners as well as her brilliance and good looks. Life on board a whaler must have presented

Whalers at Lahaina, Hawaiian Islands
Artist: Ron Druett
Notation in the Log of the *Lucy Ann*
Never happy on voyage, Martha Brown wrote in her husband's logbook, "Adieu to Whalegrounds and now for home and right glad am I. And now my Dear, alow me to inform you that this is the last time you are to leave, or visit these waters which to you have become familiar according to your own assertions. Martha." Edwin, however, disobeyed her, going on at least one more voyage.

quite a contrast to life back home, particularly in the lack of social niceties, and yet she managed to raise her daughter, Emma, on shipboard, despite the disapproval of the Hawaiian missionaries, who opined that "no one on a whaler ever knew anything." Captain Rose's style of discipline was rough and ready, too. Many years later, Emma described a time when the crew came aft to complain to Captain Jetur Rose about the quality of the food. One of the men, "a great burly fellow," emphasized his argument by hefting up a cask of butter, and throwing it overboard. Captain Rose's response was prompt. He simply stepped forward, picked up the complainant in his powerful hands, and tossed him overboard after the butter.

Obviously, this was not the way things had been back in the mansion at Water Mill (just east of Southampton) where Caroline had been raised. So why did whalemen like Rose, Jennings, White... and Edwin Brown... invite their wives along on voyage – and why did their wives consent to sail?

The answer, of course, was the terrible loneliness of the long-distance seaman. Trapped by the growing scarcity of whales into ever-lengthening voyages, the whaling masters saw all kinds of advantages in the wife-carrying fad. In January 1861, for example, when George W. Nye of the *Courser* noted that Sarah Eliza Jennings had joined her husband Captain Andrew Jennings on the *Mary Gardiner* of Sag Harbor, he made the envious comment, if only "I was Cap and had my Wife, Te Wee."

In many cases the wives, tired of years of separation, felt exactly the same way. When Emmeline Winters sailed with Jonas on the *Elizabeth Frith* in 1848, she and her husband had been together just ten months in eight years of marriage. This unnatural situation was the rule,

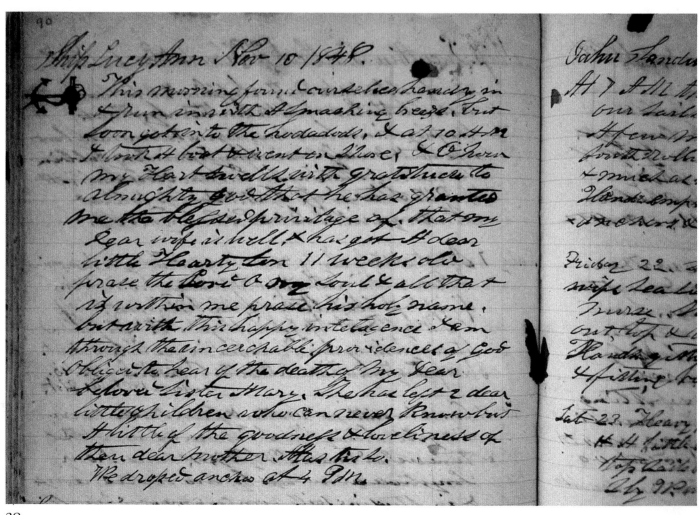

not the exception, and so, despite the risks and tragedies, the discomfort, the constant threat of seasickness, the grim nature of the trade, and the ever-increasing length of the voyages, at least twenty Long Island wives followed in the wake of Maria and Elizabeth Green, Maria Baldwin, and Mrs. Edwin Peter Brown.

It was little wonder, however, that on the homeward passage Martha Brown wrote in a space she found in the ship *Lucy Ann*'s logbook, "Adieu to Whale-grounds and now for home and right glad am I. And now my Dear," she added, "alow me to inform you that this is the last time you are to leave, or visit these waters which to you have become familliar according to your own assertions. Martha."

Captain Brown paid no heed to this, for he undertook a Cape Horn voyage in 1852, on the newly built merchant ship *Amelia*. Unsurprisingly, in the context of the time, the voyage was to California. Many of his brother whalemen had done it already, most of them in 1849. Captain Henry Green (Roxanna's husband) was one of them, going off in command of the *Sabina* with a crew of optimistic fortune-hunters, nineteen of them master mariners, so that as the vessel sailed from Sag Harbor three veteran captains and six mates could be counted aloft loosing topsails. Roxanna's fifteen-year-old nephew Charles was cabin boy, and her brother-in-law Captain Barney Green was a member of the crew.

Other vessels and other captains followed in the *Sabina*'s wake. Some of the old Sag Harbor masters – Captain George Corwin, Captain David Hand – found a last resting place in California. Others did well, but not out of gold, making their money out of selling goods to miners, and carrying them from place to place. Some, like Edwin Brown, went into the merchant trade. Brown collected a holdful of guano ("bird dung" as he called it, the accumulated deposits left by seabirds on the arid islands of the Peruvian coast) in Peru after discharging his freight at San Francisco, and then re-

turned home, but others – Lawrence Edwards, John H. Fordham – remained in the Pacific, plying the lucrative San Francisco-Shanghai route. Some returned to whaling, one of them Captain Henry Green, who took out the *Sheffield* of Cold Spring Harbor in 1854 with his wife Roxanna, on board. Few of his fellow masters emulated his example, however, and even those who did seemed half-hearted about it. Andrew Jennings, for example, was so delighted by the performance of the *Mary Gardiner* in eluding the Confederate raider that he promptly quit whaling and took up blockade-running instead.

The end of the profit in whale oil was heralded in 1859, when petroleum was first recovered in commercial quantities at Titusville, Pennsylvania, providing a potential substitute for whale oil. But already the highly profitable days of whaling which had encouraged the participation of small ports like Sag Harbor, Greenport, and Cold Spring Harbor had passed. And so, wife-carrying was a short-lived fashion. But in the meantime fascinating times and remarkable adventures had been recorded, to serve as a testimonial to these sister sailors who managed, somehow, to create a home in that most unhomelike place, a wind-propelled whaleship at sea.

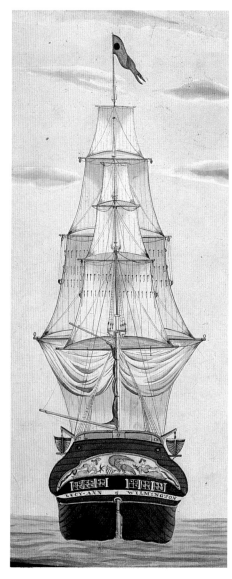

Captain Edwin Brown and whaleship *Lucy Ann* of Wilmington
c.1840
The *Lucy Ann* sailed out of Wilmington, Delaware before sailing out of Orient, Long Island in 1847. Painting by an unknown crew member. Courtesy of the Kendall Whaling Museum, Sharon, Massachusetts, USA.

Captain Edwin Brown of Orient was a very successful whaling master, taking out vessels that included the *Lucy Ann* (above), and the *Washington*, both of Greenport. Retiring from the sea a comparatively wealthy man at the age of 40, he took over management of the Orient Wharf.

ALDRICH, Martha Maria Bayles (Mrs. Herman S.), merchant brig *Atalanta* of Port Jefferson (371 tons), 1880s.

AUSTIN, Mrs. James, whaleship *William Tell* of Sag Harbor, (370 tons), 1858.

BABCOCK, Nancy Maria (Mrs. Hedges), whaleship *Caroline* of Greenport (252 tons), 1847 (possible); *Caroline* of Greenport, NY, 1850-52.

BAKER, Emma Evans (Mrs. Henry Davis), unknown Mediterranean traders, 1860s.

BALDWIN, Maria Cartwright (Mrs. Smith), whaling bark *Roanoke* of Greenport (252 tons), 1847-49; coasting schooner *Adelia Felicia* (137 tons), 1850s.

The Sister Sailors of Long Island:

A PRELIMINARY LIST, 1826-1915

BAYLES, Mary Lurch (Mrs. Edward Post), coasting schooner *Lavinia Belle* of Port Jefferson, 1903-17.

BROWN, Emily Van Dercook (Mrs. John Alexander), merchant ship *John Harvey* of New York (736 tons), 1876.

BROWN, Martha Smith Brewer (Mrs. Edwin), whaleship *Lucy Ann* of Greenport (309 tons), 1847-49.

BURTOW, Mrs., schooner *Jennie Rosaline* (348 tons), 1889 (wrecked).

CAWSE, Emma Brown (Mrs. John R.), merchant ship *John R. Worchester*, 1876-1877

CLARKE, Mrs. Robert K., merchant ship *Frank N. Thayer* of Quogue (1,647 tons), 1880s.

DAVIS, Carrie Hubbard (Mrs. Charles), of Orient, coasting schooner *Jacob S. Ellis* (12 tons); 1875-83.

DOW, Susan A. Tabor (Mrs. Lorenzo), of Orient, schooner *Odd Fellow (28 tons)*, 1870s

EDWARDS, Jane M. (Mrs. Henry H.), whaleship *Nathaniel P. Tallmadge* of Cold Spring Harbor (370 tons), 1851-55.

EDWARDS, Emeline Shepard (Mrs. Jonathan), whaleship *Ontario* of Sag Harbor (489 tons), 1850-54 (* probable, though her husband was second mate).

EDWARDS, Eliza Wheeler (Mrs. Eli), whaling bark *Black Eagle* of Sag Harbor (311 tons), 1857-58; ship *Splendid* of Cold Spring Harbor (473 tons, Capt. Samuel Pierson, Eli was first mate) 1859-60.

FARMER, Mary, 14-year-old passenger, of Mattituck, merchant bark *Nomad*, 1875.

GARDINER, Polly Hubbard (Mrs. Henry), whaleship *Dawn*, of New York, 1826

GRANT, Mrs. William James, whaleship *Huntsville* of Cold Spring (523 tons), 1854-8.

GREEN, Elizabeth Chapman (Mrs. James M.), whaling bark *Nimrod* of Sag Harbor (280 tons), 1851-53 (* probable).

GREEN, Maria E. Brown (Mrs. Barney R.), whaleship *Ontario* of Sag Harbor (489 tons), 1845-8.

GREEN, Roxanna Stewart Fordham (Mrs. Henry J.), whaleship *Sheffield* of Cold Spring (579 tons), 1854-9.

HALSEY, Melvina Terry (Mrs. Charles), whaleship *Milton* of New Bedford (388 tons), 1860-65; whaling bark *Benjamin Cummings* of New Bedford (305 tons), 1866-71.

HAWKINS, Mrs. George, merchant bark *B. F. Watson* (993 tons), 1884.

HAWKINS, Mary Ann (Mrs. William Lester), coasting schooner *Village Queen* of Stony Brook (220 tons), 1858.

HUNTTING, Caroline Hildreth (Mrs. Henry), whaleship *Jefferson* of Sag Harbor (435 tons), 1857-61 (* probable).

HUNTTING, Martha White (Mrs. James), whaleship *Jefferson* of Sag Harbor (435 tons), 1853-57 (** probable).

JAYNE, Mrs. Austin, of Setauket, merchant bark *Nomad (476 tons)*, built in Port Jefferson 1872.

JENNINGS, Ann Eliza Foster (Mrs. Andrew), whaleship *Mary Gardiner* of Sag Harbor (316 tons), 1860-61 (joined ship at St. Helena, August 29, 1860).

JENNINGS, Catherine (Mrs. Wickham), whaleship *Camillus* of Sag Harbor (345 tons), 1841-43 (* probable).

JONES, Elizabeth Evans (Mrs. Benjamin, second wife), merchant ship *Tri-Mountain* of New York (1,301 tons), 1875-6.

JONES, Mary Swift (Mrs. Benjamin, first wife), merchant bark *Mary & Louisa* of New York (497 tons), 1858-61.

KILGORE, Addie B. Winters (Mrs. William E.), Revenue Cutter *Bear*, U.S. Seal Poaching Patrol, 1870s.

LAVEY, Mrs. Eugene, coasting schooner *Nahum Chapin* (596 tons), 1897 (wrecked).

LUDLOW, Phebe (Mrs. Isaac), whaleship *Hamilton* of Sag Harbor (322 tons), 1840-2 (* probable).

LUDLOW, Sarah E. (Mrs. James), whaling bark *Union II* of Sag Harbor (300 tons), 1861-64 (* probable).

MILLER, Mary Ann Schellinger (Mrs. Davis), whaling brig *Wickford* of Sag Harbor (115 tons), 1841 (*** probable).

MULFORD, Mary Hedges (Mrs. Jeremiah), whaleship *Nathaniel P. Talmadge* of Cold Spring Harbor (370 tons), 1848-51 (* probable).

PHILLIPS, (Mrs. William), *Syren Queen* (port unknown), 1855-8.

PIERSON, Fanny (Mrs. Samuel B.), whaleship *Edgar* of Cold Spring Harbor (420 tons), 1852 (wrecked).

RAYNOR, Adelaide Robinson (Mrs. George W.), whaleship *Reindeer* of New Bedford (450 tons), 1860-65; *Reindeer* of New Bedford, 1866-69.

RAYNOR, Ettabel, Isabel, Alice, and Kathleen, daughters of Captain Eugene Raynor, coasting schooner *Ruth B. Cobb* (620 tons), ca.1910-15.

ROGERS, Adelia, passenger on whaleship *Zenas Coffin*, Captain Jetur Rose, home from Honolulu, 1856-57. Husband and ship unknown.

ROSE, Caroline Benedict (Mrs. Jetur), whaleship *Zenas Coffin* of Nantucket (368 tons), 1853-57; whaling bark *Pacific* of New Bedford (385 tons), 1862-65; whaling bark *Trident* of New Bedford (449 tons), 1865-71.

ROWLAND, Mary Satterly (Mrs. Henry), coasting schooner *Stephen H. Townsend (182 tons)*, 1852-54; merchant brig *Thomas W. Rowland* (366 tons) 1855-62; merchant bark *Glenwood*, 1862-65; brig *Mary E. Rowland* (263 tons), 1866-75.

SMITH, Cordelia (Mrs. Freeman H.), whaleship *Huntsville* of Cold Spring Harbor (523 tons), 1849-51.

SMITH, Mrs. Richard P., whaleship *Splendid* of Cold Spring Harbor (473 tons), 1851-53; whaleship *Eliza F. Mason* of New Bedford (582 tons), 1857-61.

TABOR, Carolyn Hallock Lowen (Mrs. James Madison), whaling bark *Augusta* of Sag Harbor (390 tons), 1857-61.

THOMPSON, Harriet Janette Aldrich (Mrs. James Henry), coasting schooner *Addie P. Avery* (332 tons), 1866-.

WELLS, Carrie Bantle, [Mrs. Robert Francis Wells], merchant schooners *Bertha L. Downs* and *Richard Carver* for coastal trade as well as deepwater voyage. Carrie sailed with her children, Marjorie Louise (b.1/31/1906), Caroline Adair (b. approx. 1909), and Robert Charles(b. approx. 1912).

WHITE, Elizabeth Howell (Mrs. Elias H.), whaling bark *Courser* of New Bedford (259 tons), 1871 (wrecked).

WICKS, Jemina Secord (Mrs. William Clark Horton) (ship unknown) voyage to Rio 1876.

WINTERS, Emmeline Hallock (Mrs. Jonas), whaling bark *Elizabeth Frith* of Sag Harbor (355 tons), 1848-50; whaling brig *Charlotte* II (230 tons), 1850-52.

*probability based on comparing birth dates of children with precise dates of voyages.
** probability based on documentation of a seafaring Mrs. Huntting (Christian name not stated) given by Eliza Brock of the Nantucket whaleship Lexington, June 26, 1855.
*** probability based on Davis Miller's log on the Thomas Dickason, entry dated August 23, 1840.

NOTE
This is a first attempt to quantify the seafaring women of Long Island. Obviously, it is by no means complete, as many more sailed on merchant voyages than those listed. Documentation is available from the author, who would be delighted to receive additions and corrections in care of the Three Village Historical Society, P.O. Box 76, East Setauket, NY 11733-0076, USA.

- Joan Druett

Primary Sources

Abrams, Mary Farmer. Letter to sister, September 1, 1875. Private Collection. Three Village Historical Society, East Setauket, New York.

Balano, James W., ed. *The Log of the Skipper's Wife*. Camden, ME: Down East Books, 1979.

Baldwin, Rev. Dwight. Correspondence. Mission Houses Museum, Honolulu, Hawaii.

Bayles, Edward P. Record of interview, May 21, 1893. Three Village Historical Society.

Brewster, Mary Burtch. Journals kept on *Tiger* of Stonington, Connecticut, 1845-50. Mstic Seaport Museum, Mystic, Connecticut.

Brock, Eliza. Journals kept on *Lexington* of Nantucket, 1853-56. Nantucket Historical Association, Nantucket, Massachusetts.

Brown, Captain Edwin Peter. Logbook kept on *Lucy Ann*, 1847-49. Oysterponds Historical Society, Orient, New York.

Brown, Martha Smith Brewer. Journal on the *Lucy Ann* 1847-1849. published as *She Went A Whaling*, Edited by Anne MacKay, Oysterponds Historical Society, Orient,

Davis, Carrie Hubbard. Correspondence, 1870-84. William Steeple Davis Trust, Orient, New York.

Davis, Carrie Hubbard. Diaries, 1870-81. William Steeple Davis Trust.

Essex, Fred. "A Pilgrimage Across the Pacific." Typescript. Stephen Phillips Memorial Library, Penobscot Marine Museum, Searsport, Maine.

Hawkins Association Newsletter, Setauket, New York, 13:144.

Jennings, Captain. Log book kept on *Mary Gardiner*, 1859-61. Rogers Memorial Library, Southampton, New York, microfilm copy in New Bedford Whaling Museum, New Bedford, Massachusetts.

Jones, Captain Benjamin. Letters to "sister" and "Brother Scud," June 3, 1868. Three Village Historical Society.

Jones, Elizabeth Evans. Diary on *Tri-Mountain* of New York, 1875. Three Village Historical Society.

Jones, Mary Swift. Letters, 1848-1861. Three Village Historical Society.

Jones, Walter. Local diary, kept in Setauket 1855-90. Notes of local inhabitants, mentions of Rowland and Jones families. Steve Poulos. Copy at Three Village Historical Society.

Latham, Nancy. *My Trip on the Water*. Orient, NY: Oysterponds Historical Society, 19 .

Latimer, Will. Journal kept on board of *Dawn* of New York, 1826-27. Canberra, Australia: Pacific Manuscripts Bureau, microfilmed at The Whaling Museum, Cold Spring Harbor, New York.

MacKay, Anne, ed. *She Went A-Whaling: The Journal of Martha Smith Brewer Brown*. Orient, NY: Oysterponds Historical Society, 1993, 1995.

"Maine Schooners" Sought for Inter-American Trade." Portland *(Maine) Press Herald*, July 21, 1942.

Miller, Davis E. Logbook kept on *Thomas Dickason*, 1839-41. Microfilm held at New Bedford Whaling Museum.

Morgan, Nathaniel. Journal kept on *Hannibal* of New London, 1849-50. Mystic Seaport Museum.

Morgan, Samuel Broadbent. Journal kept on *Florida* of Fairhaven, 1858-61. Typescript copy. The New Bedford Whaling Museum.

New Bedford *Whalemen's Shipping List and Merchants' Transcript*, 1843- .

Nye, George W. Logbook kept on *Courser*, 1860-64. Microfilm held at New Bedford Whaling Museum.

Obituary of Mrs. Jonas Winters. Sag Harbor *Express*, March 17, 1904.

Obituary of Caroline M. (Tabor) Lowen. Sag Harbor *Express*, May 18, 1905.

Pulsifer, Freeman. Travel diary, 1859-60. Peabody Essex Museum, Salem, Massachusetts.

Raynor, Ettabel. Journal kept on *Ruth B. Cobb*, 1915. Private collection. Copy at Three Village Historical Society.

Rose, Caroline and Emma. Notations in log of ship *Trident* of New Bedford, Captain Jetur Rose, log-keeper Melvin Halsey, 1865-68. Rogers Memorial Library. Microfilm at New Bedford Whaling Museum.

Rowland, Mary. Journal kept on brig *Mary E. Rowland*, January to May 1867. Three Village Historical Society.

Rowland, Mary. Letter to "My Dear Child" dated March 9, 1871, at Charleston. Three Village Historical Society.

Rowland, Mary. Letter to sister Hannah Smith, January 1873. Private collection. Copy at Three Village Historical Society.

Rowland, Mary. Memorandum of voyages from 1852-1862. Carl H. Fowler. Three Village Historical Society.

Rowland, Mary. Sea letter to sister Hannah, February 10 - April 12, 1870. Three Village Historical Society.

Rowland, Mary. Sea letters to Children, 1866-69. Private collection. Copy at Three Village Historical Society.

Rowland, Mary. Single diary entry at sea, July 8, 1869; memorandum dated Babylon, February 24, 1886, with memorandum of husband's death.

Rowland, Mary. Journal kept on brig *Thomas W. Rowland*, 1855-57. Three Village Historical Society.

Smith, Egbert Bull. *Voyage of the Two Sisters*. New York, author, 1908.

Terry, Constance J., ed. *In the Wake of Whales: The Whaling Journals of Capt. Edwin Peter Brown 1841-1847*. Orient, NY: Old Orient Press, 1988.

Wheldon, Clara. Letters written on *John Howland* of New Bedford, 1864-71 (discontinuous). New Bedford Whaling Museum.

Secondary Sources

Albion, Robert G., William A. Baker, and Benjamin W. Labaree. *New England and the Sea*. Mystic, CT: Mystic Seaport Museum, 1972.

Armbruster, Eugene L. *Brooklyn's Eastern District*. Brooklyn, NY: author, 1942.

Ashley, Clifford W. *The Yankee Whaler*. Boston: Houghton Mifflin, 1926.

Bailey, Paul. *Long Island: A History of Two Great Counties, Nassau & Suffolk*. New York: Lewis Historical Publishing, 1949.

Bayles, Richard M.. *Historical and Descriptive Sketches of Suffolk County*. 1873.

Biggins, Patricia. "Doughnuts in the Tryworks." *The Log Of Mystic Seaport* 27:1 (May 1975): 8-16.

Bonham, Julia C. "Feminist and Victorian: The Paradox of the American Seafaring Woman of the Nineteenth Century." *The American Neptune* 37:3 (July 1977): 203-18.

Bordages, Asa. "Women Against the Sea." Series in the New York *World-Telegram*. May 16, 1934 (Brown story), May 18, 1934 (Clarke story).

Bowker, Francis E. *Hull-Down*. New Bedford, MA.: author, 1963.

Brady, Elizabeth Burns. "Shelter Island and the Whaling Industry." *Old Whalers' Festival Program*, Sag Harbor, 1968.

Clinton, Audrey. "At Home at Sea," in two parts: "Whaling Wives," and "Clipper Ship Days." series in *Newsday*, March 1 and March 2, 1961.

Cluff, John A. "A New England Seafaring Family." *American Neptune* 19:2 (April 1959): 140.

Colby, Barnard L. *Whaling Captains of New London County Connecticut: For Oil and Buggy Whips*. Mystic, CT: Mystic Seaport Museum, 1990.

DePauw, Linda G. *Seafaring Women*. Boston: Houghton Mifflin, 1982.

Dodge, Ernest Stanley. "The Last Days of Coasting on Union River Bay." *American Neptune* 9:3 (July 1949): 169-79.

Druett, Joan, ed. *"She Was a Sister Sailor": The Whaling Journals of Mary Brewster, 1845-1851*. (Mystic, CT: Mystic Seaport Museum, 1992.)

Druett, Joan. *Captain's Daughter, Coasterman's Wife: Carrie Hubbard Davis of Orient*. Orient, NY: Oysterponds Historical Society, 1995.

Druett, Joan. *Petticoat Whalers*. Auckland, NZ: Collins, 1992.

Druett, Joan. "More Decency and Order: Women and Whalemen in the Pacific." *The Log of Mystic Seaport* 39:2 (Summer 1987): 65-74.

Druett, Joan. "Rough Medicine: Doctoring the Whalemen." *The Dukes County Intelligencer* 30:2 (November 1988): 3-15.

Druett, Joan. "Those Female Journals." *The Log of Mystic Seaport* 40 (Winter 1989): 115-25.

Dulles, Foster Rhea. *America in the Pacific: A Century of Expansion*. Boston: Houghton Mifflin, 1938.

Edwards, Everett, and Jeannette Edwards Rattray. *Whale Off*. New York: Coward-McCann, 1926.

Federal Writers Project. *Whaling Masters*. 1938; reprint, San Bernadino, CA: Borgo Press, 1987.

Finckenor, George A. *Whales and Whaling*. Sag Harbor, NY, 1975.

Garner, Stanton, ed. *"The Captain's Best Mate": The Journal of Mary Chipman Lawrence on the Whaler "Addison" 1856-1860*. (Providence, RI: Brown University Press, 1966).

Greer, Richard A. "Honolulu in 1847." *Hawaiian Journal of History* 4 (1970): 59-95.

Langdon, Robert. *American Whalers and Traders in the Pacific: A Guide to Records on Microfilm*. Canberra, Australia: Pacific Manuscripts Bureau, Australian National University, 1978.

Leavitt, John F. *Wake of the Coasters*. Mystic, CT: Mystic Seaport Museum, 1970, 1984.

Mallman, Rev. Jacob E. *Historical Papers on Shelter Island and its Presbyterian Church*. New York: author, 1899.

Morgan, Charles. "New England Coasting Schooners." *American Neptune* 23:1, (January 1963): 5-21.

Morris, Paul C., *American Sailing Coasters of the North Atlantic*. Chardon, OH: Bloch and Osborn 1973.

Overton, Jacqueline, *Long Island's Story*. New York: Doubleday, 1929.

Parker, Lt. W. J. Lewis, *The Great Coal Schooners of New England 1870-1909*. (Mystic, CT: Maritime Historical Association, 1948).

Portrait and Biographical Record of Suffolk County. New York: Chapman Publishing, 1896.

Rattray, Jeannette Edwards. "Long Island Women and Whaling." *New York Folklore Quarterly* (Summer, 1954).

Robinson, Edith Derby, "Mutiny on the Thayer." *Long Island Forum*, (May 1941): 107-8.

Schmitt, Frederick P. *Mark Well the Whale: Long Island Ships to Distant Seas*. Port Washington, NY: Kennikat Press, 1971.

Sherman, Stuart. *Whaling Logbooks and Journals 1613-1927: An Inventory*. revised by Judith M. Downey and Virginia M. Adams. New York: Garland Publishing, Inc., 1986.

Sleight, Harry D. *The Whale Fishery on Long Island*. Bridgehampton, NY: Hampton Press, 1931.

Starbuck, Alexander. *History of the American Whale Fishery*. 1878; reprint New York: Castle Books, 1989.

Strong, Kate W. "Down to the Sea in Ships." *Long Island Forum* (October 1956): 187-88.

Strong, Kate Wheeler. "The Bark *Mary and Louise*." *Long Island Forum*, (December 1954): 235.

Valentine, Andrus T. "'Big Manuel,' Whaling Captain." *Long Island Forum* (March 1954): 49, 56-58.

Wallace, Mary Anne. *Days of Joy and Fear: Nineteenth Century New England Family Life at Sea*. Thesis, University of Southern Maine, 1993.

Wasson, George S. *Sailing Days on the Penobscot*. New York: W.W. Norton, 1949.

Zaykowski, Dorothy Ingersoll. *Sag Harbor: The Story of an American Beauty*. New York: Sag Harbor Historical Society, Sag Harbor, New York, 1991.

Illustration Credits

Page 10:
1. William Steeple Davis Trust.

Page 11:
1. William Steeple Davis Trust.
2. Raymond Rowland Randall.
3. Collection, Three Village Historical Society.

Page 12:
1. Raymond Rowland Randall.
2. Raynor Collection, Three Village Historical Society.

Page 13:
1-3. William Steeple Davis Trust.

Page 14:
1-3. William Steeple Davis Trust.

Page 15:
1-2. William Steeple Davis Trust.

Page 16:
1,3-4. Raynor Collection, Three Village Historical Society
2. Courtesy of Carol Collins. Photographed by Parashoot, Stony Brook, New York.

Page 17:
1-3. Raynor Collection, Three Village Historical Society.

Page 18 & 19:
1. Courtesy of Dr. Sherman Mills. Photographed by Island Color, St. James, New York.

Page 20:
1. National Martitime Museum, San Francisco
2. Ron Druett.

Page 21:
1. Courtesy of the Balano Family.
2. Raynor Collection, Three Village Historical Society.

Page 22:
1. Raymond Rowland Randall.
2. Ron Druett.

Page 23:
1. Marjorie Wells Elsebough Collection
2. Delforge Family Collection.

Page 24:
1-3. Raymond Rowland Randall. Photographed by Steve Petegorsky.

Page 25:
1-2. William Leonhart Collection, Arthur M.Sackler Gallery, Smithsonian Institution

Page 26:
1. Beverly C. Tyler Collection.
2. Delforge Family Collection.

Page 27:
1-2. Collection,Three Village Historical Society. Photographed by Parashoot.

Page 28:
1-3. William Steeple Davis Trust. Photographed by Island Color.
4. Raymond Rowland Randall

Page 29:
1-2. Delforge Family Collection.

Page 30:
1. Ron Druett.

Page 31:
1. Captain Henry Gardiner Family Collection.

Page 32:
1-2. Captain Henry Gardiner Family Collection.
3. Mystic Seaport Museum, Mystic, CT.

Page 33:
1. Audrey Hauck.

Page 34:
1. Ron Druett.

Page 35:
1. William Steeple Davis Trust.

Page 36:
1. Oysterponds Historical Society.

Page 37:
1. Southampton Colonial Society.
2. Ron Druett.

Page 38:
1. Ron Druett
2. Reproduced courtesy of Janet T. Swanson & Oysterponds Historical Society.

Page 39:
1. Oysterponds Historical Society.
2. The Kendall Whaling Museum, Sharon, Massachusetts, USA.

Front Cover:
1. Three Village Historical Society
2. Raymond Rowland Randall
3. Courtesy of Dr. Sherman Mills

Back Cover:
1. William Steeple Davis Trust

Index